THE GOULDIAN
FINCH HANDBOOK

THE GOULDIAN FINCH HANDBOOK:

Feeding, Housing, and Breeding the
Lady Gouldian Finch

The Ultimate Owner's Guide You Didn't Know You Needed

TANYA LOGAN

Finch Hollow Press
Florida, USA

Copyright © 2020 Tanya Logan.

All rights reserved. No part of this publication may be reproduced, distributed, or transmitted in any form or by any means, including photocopying, recording, or other electronic or mechanical methods, without the prior written permission of the publisher, except in the case of brief quotations embodied in critical reviews and certain other noncommercial uses permitted by copyright law.

ISBN: 978-1-7358328-0-7 (Paperback)

Library of Congress Control Number: 1735832804

Cover by Rica Cabrex
Design by Rica Cabrex

Finch Hollow Press, Florida 2020.

www.GouldianGardens.com and www.TanyaLogan.com.

Disclaimer

While the publisher and author have used their best efforts in preparing this book, they make no representations or warranties with respect to the accuracy or completeness of the contents of the book. Specifically, they disclaim any implied warranties of fitness for a particular purpose. No warranty may be created or extended by sales representatives or written sales materials. The advice and strategies contained herein may not be suitable for your situation. You should consult with a professional when appropriate, particularly with a certified avian veterinarian when dealing with illness or diet. Neither the publisher nor the author shall be liable for any loss of profit or damages including but not limited to special, incidental, consequential, personal or other damages.

Table of Contents

Introduction: Who Is This Finch, Anyway? ix

Chapter 1: Becoming a Bird Slave 1
Chapter 2: I Prefer Ranch Style With a Pool -
The Gouldian Home. 21
Chapter 3: Where Shall We Put the TV? -
Cage Accessories. 51
Chapter 4: I Eat Like a Bird - Feeding the
Lady Gouldian 58
Chapter 5: 1+1 Soon Equals a Flock -
Breeding. 113
Chapter 6: Eggs, Anyone? 135
Chapter 7: Egg and Baby Problems 151
Chapter 8: Does That Come in Pink? Genetics. . 185
Chapter 9: I Don't Feel Like School Today. 199
Chapter 10: Lists of 10. 248

End 268
Acknowledgements. 269
About the Author. 270
Appendix A: Glossary 271
Appendix B: An Endangered Species 273
Appendix C: Timing for Full Spectrum Lighting. . 275
Appendix D: Forms And Documents 277
Bibliography. 281
Endnotes 285

Introduction

WHO IS THIS FINCH, ANYWAY?

And Who is this Author?

For a writer, there is a natural flow from learning about something to writing about it. Once I had become a keeper of Gouldian Finches, it was only natural that I share them with others. They're so delightfully colored and have pleasing little sounds – who wouldn't want to share?

To allow the reader to read without clicking away from the text at every turn, I've created a webpage with links to all the items and products mentioned, as well as more photos. Please visit https://GouldianGardens.com/book_links to download a pdf file that can be printed out or saved on your computer. It will be updated periodically, so if your copy is out-of-date you can grab a new one.

It is with great pleasure that I present this book to the public. It has been more than 3 years in the making. I am not a veterinarian or even an expert; I am a Gouldian finch enthusiast and aviculturist, a keeper of birds. I have written the book based on my own experience and that of many others, as well as deep and thorough research.

The world of Lady Gouldian finches is beautiful and complex. Lady Gouldians are known throughout the world for their vibrant color; they are also known, whether correctly or not, for being difficult to raise. Let me emphasize that my methods of care are based *on my own results*. Yours may be different from mine. There can be a thousand reasons why a procedure works for one person and not the next; it's not my intent to show every scenario, just to share mine.

I pray that you will find this handbook useful and informative, and that you are able to keep your Gouldians in fantastic condition.

The Lady Gouldian Finch

For ease, I will use the term Gouldian Finch, or simply Gouldian, to refer to the Lady Gouldian Finch. It is also known as Rainbow Finch and Painted Finch (although, to confuse matters further, there is another finch with that moniker).

I fell in love the first time with Gouldians because of their bright, beautiful colors. I fell for them all over again once I owned a few and discovered their delightful personality. They are comical, interactive, and gentle. They do not peck at each other overly much, and will learn to greet their owner each morning. Their sounds are soft "yoo-hoos" and quiet songs. They are intensely interested in what's going on around them. What could be more enjoyable and relaxing than watching an aviary filled with these beautiful creatures?

Because of their gentle nature and vibrant colors, Gouldian finches have become my favorite hobby. I enjoy sitting by the aviary and listening to their songs and calls and breeding them to share with others. I have written this book in hopes that you, too will enjoy a life with the gentle song of the Gouldian finches.

The book was nearly complete when I made two important decisions. The first was to create a front section for each chapter that is a sort of fast-forward guide to Gouldian ownership. That is because many people purchase finches on a whim, and they have no idea what to do with them. They need answers *now*-- they don't have time to read a whole book. It can be used first, or skipped over altogether.

The downside of creating a fast-forward guide is that if one reads the entire book in order, it may seem that some information is repeated. I have tried to keep that to a minimum. You will find *Lists of 10s* in the back, which provide some quick tips and tricks as well.

The other big decision is the medical chapter. I originally wrote every technique I use or heard about using to sustain Gouldian health, but I'm not a veterinarian. I worried about legal issues. So I removed it all, changing to a lighter-weight "here's what you might do" guide. But that was taking it painfully close to all those other books, the ones that don't tell you what to do when your bird is ill.

Finally, I settled on a format sharing what your veterinarian might do in a given situation. You will have a double advantage. You'll be employing the expertise of an avian vet while being able to glance back at the book and be confident in the direction your vet goes. Plus as a bonus I'm including many natural remedies for readers who prefer not to use chemicals on their birds.

I hope you enjoy this book as much as I've enjoyed writing it!

Distribution and Habitat

Finches are found in every part of the world. All fall under the order *passeriformes*, so we refer to them as passerines. Technically passerines are perching birds; they have four toes, three that face forward and the other one backward. More often you'll hear them referred to as "songbirds." There are 5,400 types of bird in that order--more than half of all birds.

The Lady Gouldian finch, or *Erythrura gouldiae*, originates from the grassy plains of northern Australia. The finches migrate south to breed, roughly September through March, and return north again afterward.

Northern Australia's climate is subtropical, with temperatures ranging from 70F (21C) to 91F (33C). Humidity levels range from 60% during the dry season to over 80% during the wet season. The open woodlands and grassland areas create a perfect environment for wrens and finches, of which there are many.

The Gouldian Finch as a caged bird can be traced back to the 1880s in both Germany and Australia. Even then, the species was reputed to be challenging to keep and breed. They spread to England, and eventually were brought to the U.S.

Unfortunately, whenever there is beauty in nature it invariably falls prey to the greed of mankind; herein enters the market for caged birds and the industry driving it via bird trapping. Lady Gouldian finches were trapped by the thousands between 1958 and 1981. Australia placed a ban on the export of native birds in 1960.

The correlated number of sightings by ornithologists in Australia's Northern Territory dropped from thousands in the 1960s to very few in the 1980s, in spite of the ban. This is thought to be from disease as well as habitat changes. In 1982, the Gouldian became fully protected and in 1992, it became classified as "endangered in the wild." There are recovery plans in place for efforts to increase the Gouldian population in Australia.

Today in the United States we are only allowed to keep non-native species. Birds that are found anywhere in North America may not be kept as pets, including the American goldfinch. Fortunately, Gouldians are non-native.

Gouldians are not a colony bird in the wild. During the breeding season, each nest can be found miles from the next family of Gouldians. When it is not the breeding season, wild Gouldian finches can be found in mixed flocks with other finches. In a captive situation it is perfectly acceptable to keep several pairs of Gouldians together. We may also follow this example and provide them companionship in the form of other varieties of finches-- just be sure to check the compatibility list in the back of this book to ensure the finches you have selected are compatible with Gouldians.

The Gouldian, as any finch owner has already discovered, is one of the most trusting species we can own. Although not usually kept for hand-taming, once Gouldians are used to their owner's movements around the cage or aviary, they become calm in his or her presence. I have one male that sits on the lowest perch and sings to me, and others that respond to their names. My favorite male, Jazz, always twists his head upside down to look at me when I speak to him. Perhaps he believes we'd look better standing on our heads.

Coloration

The normal or wild-type male Gouldian finch will be just over 5 inches long (about 135 mm). He will weigh about 16 g. His main body color is olive green, although you may notice some brown feathers on the wings. There is a turquoise band around his head that extends up into the crown. Beside that band is a narrow black line that goes around the head, which is broader under the chin. The beak is ivory with a red tip. The chest is bright purple. The abdomen area is bright yellow. Under the tail is

Figure 1-1 Normal Male Gouldian. © Tina Billings 2020.

light blue; the tail itself is a dark blue. His 2 pintail wires are fairly long. His mask will be either black or red, although red is the true wild type. Black was at some point a mutation but is often seen in the wild.

The normal or wild-type hen is about 4 3/4 inches long (130 mm), and weighs about 16 grams. One thing I like about the Gouldian Finch is that the females, unlike some other species, still carry a great deal of color on their own. They are not drab by any means.

Her body color is olive green. Her red mask might be a slightly duller

Figure 1-2 Normal Female Gouldian. Note the lighter breast color.
© Lisa Judson-Bohard 2020.

shade of red than the male's, with a thicker black band around it. The breast is light purple. The beak is light gray with a red tip. Her abdomen is a lighter, lemony yellow. Her undertail is off-white, and the tail is shorter than the male's with shorter tail wires. Occasionally a hen might have two longer wires (pintail feathers), almost like a male's.

Aside from the 'normal' green-backed Gouldian, there are variations, which are called mutations. The back-color mutations are presently as follows:

- Yellow
- Blue
- Pastel

- Lutino
- Albino

There are other colors that have appeared in the past, and I am sure there will be more in the future. One more "color" bears mention, and that is the melanistic Gouldian finch, which is not a color mutation at all as some believe, but rather a deficiency in lighting, iron, or vitamins. It is thought that one or all of these deficiencies cause the darker feathers, which may appear anywhere on the body. Here we are not referring to the black outline around a red-masked finch, which is normal, but some black feathering on the body, often extending over the entire body. With proper care, the feathers will most likely return to a normal color at the next molt.

Breast colors

We discussed the purple breast, which is dominant. There are two more: the white breast and a lilac mutation. Lilac is not a diluted purple or a cross-dominance between purple and white. Instead, it is a color that can stand on its own. There is mention of pink and blue breasts, but those are not prevalent here in the U.S.

Figure 1-3 Purple Breast Male

Figure 1-4 White Breast Male

Masks

There are three mask (head) colors that may appear In Gouldian finches: red, black, and yellow, which expresses itself as orange. You will also see a straw-colored head, which is covered in the chapter on breeding (straw being the red mask). And to make matters more confusing, a yellow-backed black head has a visual white head.

Figure 1-5 Mask Colors

Color Shorthand

When discussing Gouldians in writing on the Internet, one might come across something like this: RHPBGB. Translated, this is a bird that has a red head, purple breast, and green back -- a "normal" Gouldian. When using this shorthand, always mention head color first, followed by breast color. Back color is last. Some will refer to orange head, but the proper term is yellow (YH).

Fledgling and Juvenile Colors

If your new Gouldians breed, you may be surprised at the appearance of the babies. Newly hatched finches are pink-skinned and have no feathers at all. After they feather in, they look sort of grayish with olive green backs and tail feathers. The beak will be blackish, maybe with a red tip. Legs and feet are a tan to pink color. All in all, they're boring compared to their brightly colored parents!

One trait of Australian cavity nesting finches is that they will have several tubercles beside their beak. These are often described as phosphorescent, although that is incorrect. They reflect light, they don't luminesce on their own. These help the parents find the babies' beaks for feeding inside the dark nest cavity. There is no need for you to do anything about these tubercles; as the baby ages, they will disappear.

Figure 1-6 Baby Gouldian and Parents. Author's collection.

When the babies are 3 to 8 months old, they will begin to molt. At that time, the adult coloration will appear – that of the parents or the mutation they will be. Many breeders claim they can tell the color from early on. Sometimes the color can be predicted with a genetic calculator. Sometimes you won't know its color until the baby is molted out. Even experienced breeders sometimes get a surprise; for example, they believe a head to be black, but at the age of six months they spot a red feather – it's going to be a redhead!

Figure 1-7 Tubercles on young Gouldian. Author's collection.

One tricky color factor is when a hen is yellow backed. If she is going to be a yellow head, you won't really see this until well into or after the first molt, when her head shows just a touch of peach fluff. This is part of what makes breeding Gouldian finches so much fun.

Taxonomy

Scientific Classification

Kingdom	Animalia
Phylum	Cordata
Class	Aves
Order	Passeriformes
Family	Estrildidae
Genus	Erythrura
Species	*E. Gouldia*

Cloebia Gouldiae Gouldiae is also correct.

1 Becoming a Bird Slave

10 Easy Facts about Being Owned by Lady Gouldian Finches

1. They require a cage of about 30" x 18" x 18"
2. Besides the cage, you need lighting (if no access to sunlight), food, vitamins, and cage accessories.
3. They must be kept in pairs, never singly, but a pair can be two males or two hens.
4. Their diet consists primarily of seeds and pellets along with salad-like vegetables -- the more the better.
5. They are sexually dimorphic, meaning you can tell the males from the females by their color.
6. They are quiet and will not bother the neighbors.
7. They are more laid-back than many types of finches.
8. They are safe for mixed species aviaries*
9. If you supply a nest, they will breed! If you don't want to breed them, don't give them a nest.
10. They live an average of eight years; many live much longer.

*See the Appendix for a list of birds that mix well with Gouldians.

Purchasing a Finch

There's a cardinal rule to pet ownership, and that is: Do not ever buy a pet on a whim. This goes double for birds, as they are not the easiest pets to keep by far. They live longer than many 4-legged species, and they're messier and more time-consuming. Many people assume they can 'get rid of' birds easily if they no longer want them, but it is much more difficult to sell them, or even give them away, than one would imagine. Bird rescues are filled to the brim, and I see "free" ads for finches every day on Craigslist. Gouldian finches can live ten years or more, so that purchase is a 10-year commitment.

If you have decided to own a Lady Gouldian finch, kudos to you for doing your research first. It is best to purchase your cage and other supplies **before** buying a finch; if you haven't already done so read the next section, Cage and Accessories, to be fully prepared before your bird's arrival. Too many of us have purchased a bird and carried it along to the local pet store to grab a cage and accessories; we end up with things that are not the best choices for our pets, and some can be downright dangerous.

How to Select a Lady Gouldian Finch

The Lady Gouldian finch is about 5 to 5-1/2 inches long and is sexually dimorphic, meaning you can visually tell males from females. Males have the brighter colors, although females are certainly not drab - that's actually one of my favorite characteristics of the Gouldian, that the female is beautiful in her own right.

If possible when shopping for your finch, spend a great deal of time observing. Look for bright eyes, an alert behavior, and smooth feathers. On a healthy finch, there are no bare spots in the feathers. The beak should be smooth and straight, with no overlapped or scissor tips. Legs and feet are smooth skin with no lumps.

In addition, observe the finches in the same cage and in nearby cages. Are they also healthy and alert? Do any seem lethargic or sport bald patches? Are any beaks or feet misshapen?

Lastly, consider the history of their care, which is exhibited by the state of the cage. Perches and cage floors should be relatively free of droppings; water should be fresh and clear. The food dishes may be in a bit of disarray, especially if it's later in the day, but they should not be contaminated with droppings or debris. If all these factors seem good, then it is safe to purchase the finch.

As you are shopping for your first finches, these are merely details to keep in mind. If you find a bird that's outside the norm--only 4 inches long, or sitting lethargically on a perch--don't buy it. A bird kept in dirty conditions may harbor parasites that will cause long-term health problems, or he may already be ill (birds hide illness *really* well). Don't buy it to 'save' it either; move on to find a healthy bird that you can enjoy.

Birds can be obtained from a private breeder, a show, or a pet store. It is good to keep in mind that at pet stores or fairs, finches have been exposed to two potentially detrimental factors: Illness and stress. This does not mean you should *never* buy from these venues, but it does mean one should carefully treat the incoming pet for parasites and disease, and quarantine as necessary.

Buying at Fairs

Bird shows or fairs are a good place to find suppliers, even if one is uncomfortable purchasing them at the show itself. Most vendors are honest, and if the host is a local club you can get recommendations from their members. Although crowded conditions (for both you and the birds) make it difficult to spend much time watching their behavior, there is usually a wide variety to choose from with several different Gouldian vendors. All birds at fairs are nervous, having been pulled from their natural environment, so it is impossible to learn too much by watching. At the least it is a good place to talk with breeders and collect their cards for future reference.

Do not be afraid to approach large commercial breeders who have hundreds of finches. If conditions are clean and the breeder is in the business because he/she is a fancier, chances are the birds are some of the healthiest around.

Here in Florida there is a wealth of bird fairs. Buyers are so eager that in many cases there are guards at the doors prior to the opening hour to keep them out! Many other states also have such shows, especially in locations where there are bird clubs.

But there are down sides to every situation, and purchasing at a fair can be a somewhat risky venture. Having participated in a few myself, I've learned that there are unscrupulous sellers whose stock regularly die only a few days after the purchase. Yet somehow, they manage to stay in business.

Another problem is that you can't see the true living conditions; signs of illness or parasites won't be present. You may even be purchasing a bird that has been handed off a couple of times that very day, which adds an incredible amount of stress. Lastly, you may be sold "breeding stock" that in fact is well past its prime.

One problem at bird marts is the buyer who travels hundreds of miles to purchase a specific gender, only to end up with the wrong one. This is probably not done intentionally; instead, the seller has so many finches he cannot know them all. He has not stood in the bird area observing to see whether it sings (male) or has other gender-related behaviors. Nonetheless, it is incredibly disheartening when the buyer gets back home and realizes the new hen is really a lavender-breasted male.

If I were to buy Gouldians at a show, I would probably visit several shows in the area first and get to know the vendors. Once I had their trust, I would start asking who THEY would buy from; in this way, without insulting a fellow vendor, they can point you in the right direction. Perform the same checks and observations as listed above--with the understanding that at a bird fair, finches are especially nervous and their behavior may not be characteristic of their normal personality.

Buying from a Pet Store

A few pet stores may have Gouldians in stock, with prices generally being higher than the norm. Some pet stores may not carry Gouldians, but are able to order them. Pet stores are looked at in a negative light where birds are concerned, but if the store is clean and the bird area contains perches, swings, fresh food and water, and the cages are not overcrowded, it might be a good place to purchase. Be sure to ask about their guarantee. Take note of how many employees are well versed in bird knowledge -- you may need to confer with them later. Also take a look at their supplies. Do they carry finch-specific food and supplies? If not, where are you planning to get them?

A pet peeve of mine is when people purchase a finch from a pet store or a vendor at a flea market claiming they "rescued" it from its horrible conditions. No, this bird was a purchase, and the sale gave the seller success--so they will bring in more birds to sell!

People who are concerned about the conditions would be better served to visit the local humane society and make a report. Buying a sick or malnourished finch may seem noble, but it is a risky purchase, and might carry illness to the home flock.

Buying Online

Buying online is an option that was omitted from the above list. That's because, if this is your first foray into finches, Internet purchases are best avoided. People who purchase online are buying blind with no knowledge of the seller or his birds. The history and health are unknown. Sellers often lie to buyers about the age and even the sex of finches if they can get away with it. *I have had it happen to me.* For first Gouldians, please try not to buy over the Internet. If you must, then at least ask for professional references and check them, and get all the details of the sale in writing, especially if they ask to be paid via an app.

If I were starting over and had no finches, I would find a local breeder, probably a smaller breeder with fewer birds. Someone who knows their birds well, and probably names them. Someone who is knowledgeable about health, care, and hygiene, and willing to spend time educating buyers. I would make sure that at least two people had told me this is a reputable breeder with no known problems in his/her flock.

I would visit this person's aviary a couple of times and choose two or three prospects as my next bird. I then would stand and observe those finches for a period of time -- an hour, if the owner allowed. Watching, listening, looking, comparing.

What Am I Looking For?

- Healthy, active birds. Curious and intelligent, they notice you and may even approach the bars to look at you. They have bright, clean, alert eyes with no crust or discharge whatsoever. They appear sleek, with the feathers held against the body as a unit; their outline is smooth. Wings fold over the back evenly with no crossing or drooping. The feathers should be clean all over. Movements are made easily with no lameness or lack of balance.
- When the bird breathes, there should be absolutely no tail-bobbing (with the breath). No panting, unless it is outdoors and the temperatures are extremely hot--and then only occasionally. No nasal discharge. No clicking noise should accompany the breathing.
- The droppings should be well formed into a spiral type shape, and are made of three parts: dark green, white, and a little clear water.(You will only see the water if the dropping is super-fresh) Droppings that are runny, yellow, or dark brown indicate illness.
- *What if I am new to finches, and to Lady Gouldians,* you ask. I would ask and ask questions. The breeder will probably be glad to answer them, and hap-

py to connect you with healthy finches--perhaps even some of his favorites. He may also offer you a health guarantee, although whether he does is not an indication of his reliability as a breeder.

Good To Know:

- Some breeders have a policy of not allowing visitors into their aviculture area. This is not a "red flag" or an indicator for you to move on to another breeder; it is how they prevent disease from being carried in, and how they prevent theft of their flock.
- Visiting shows and pet shops can help teach you to recognize differences in beak color, molt or feather conditions, and what normal behavior is for a Lady Gouldian finch. This way *you* will know you're buying healthy stock.
- If you have owned parrots in the past, getting a finch is like starting over. They're completely different.
- Never own a single Gouldian. These are flock animals that do best in a social setting, so purchase 2 at the minimum. They can be the same sex or opposite sex.
- Always purchase birds that are past their first molt. Otherwise they can become "stuck in molt" and keep their olive coat, or part of it, for as long as a year before finally getting adult feathers.

NOTE:

Some fanciers have said they would never purchase a finch without handling it first. I, on the other hand, would never sell to someone who wanted to handle my birds! So I guess we don't have a meeting of the minds. Here are my reasons for not letting a potential buyer touch them, and why I don't think this is a red flag for buyers:

- They are easily stressed, and handling them may make them more so. Stress can lead to illness or even quick death. Why risk that? Even a buyer should want them to be as calm as possible for the transaction.
- Additionally, I don't know what OTHER birds that buyer may have handled. Or whether he has an illness that can be passed to birds. He/she may transmit germs into my cages, causing potentially fatal illness.
- If we are at a show, every time the cage door is open we run the risk of a bird escaping. Once they're loose, there is almost no chance of catching them. I can't trust someone I don't know to cover the door properly, so I am not allowing anyone at all, except myself, to open the doors.

What it's Like To Live with Lady Gouldians

Many people get into finches believing in one or more fallacies. For example, they think they are an easy or beginner bird which they can be given away if it doesn't work out. Or that people just have finches for display, with no interaction. Or that they will not be as smart as bigger birds they've had in the past. The majority of people seem to believe that finches only live a couple of years. None of these myths are true.

Gouldians are calm compared to other finches, but they may seem somewhat flighty if you've never had birds before. They make terrific companions. They have exceptionally soft songs and calls. They recognize their human companions and will come to the cage bars to listen, cocking their heads this way and that as if they understand every word. They'll also give a little show, singing for you so you'll say, "good bird." I have one male in a colony cage that hops onto a certain swing and sings to me every single time I walk toward the cage. Mine constantly amaze me with their curiosity and intelligence.

In planning for their lifespan, the average is eight years, but some have lived over twenty years. So in no way are they "beginner" (throwaway) birds. In my opinion, there is no such thing as a beginner bird.

On the flip side, some people say Gouldians are not good 'first birds,' but I believe with diligence and care they are acceptable as first birds. Some of the concerns about their delicacy are true, many are unwarranted, and others can be overcome through good husbandry.

General Behavior

Finch behavior can give you many hours of entertainment--they're much more interesting than television! They fly from perch to perch, interact with one another, and build nests if you provide a basket or box and nesting material (don't do this if you are not prepared to deal with babies).

Gouldians need plenty of exercise for good health. Flying keeps them healthy. Some finch owners provide an aviary or give them out-of-cage flying time. They are very pleasing to watch.

In the wild, Gouldians are *granivores* -- seed eaters, so feed them seeds, readily available at your local pet store, as well as fresh greens, pellet food, and eggfood. Supplementing the diet in this way produces strong, healthy birds. See Chapter 3, Feeding the Lady Gouldian, for more information, and my book *Feeding Finches.*

When kept in a clean environment, they are not prone to a lot of diseases. Mites or overgrown nails or beaks are usually the extent of it, and those can be easily prevented or remedied.

Finches are generally not hand tamed. Some people do manage to tame them, but it is rare. Most will immediately revert to wildness, even if you have hand fed them as babies. It has been suggested that getting a finch that's just fledged (left the nest) will make it more likely to become tame. I was told that one can tame it by offering millet and by holding your hand still, letting the bird approach you.

I have my hands in cages every day, and I don't see any bird wanting to approach me. I do have friends who purchase baby birds as early as 10 days, and they hand-raise and tame those. We will cover how to do that in the breeding section.

Recently some videos have surfaced showing Lady Gouldian finches saying words. I have many other species that speak, and I can tell you this: They only talk if they want to. So like any other bird, don't get a Gouldian finch with the idea of 'teaching' it to talk or taming it.

Birds in the home

The Lady Gouldian Finch is not considered a songbird because it doesn't make much noise. This is ideal for people living in apartments or smaller homes -- or who have family members that don't really want pet birds.

Besides being quiet, most people say they are also easy to keep. That is deceptive, though, because there is always cleaning to be done in the bird's quarters. We have chosen to take these beings that can fly a hundred miles in a day and confine them to a cage--therefore, we must take responsibility to clean their mess. This mess can be complicated by the presence of pets or young children. Let's discuss some solutions to this very real problem.

Clean-up

Because finches live confined to their cage or aviary, one would think there would not be a great deal of mess out of the cage. Finches are messy, and there is a lot of clean-up involved in their upkeep. They fling seed and seed hulls. They splash water out of the cage. You find feathers in corners and on the floor. If flying free, there will be droppings on the furniture and the floor, and maybe your hair. Their cages must be scrubbed and papers changed every day. Finches are probably not the pet for people who can't stand a mess. Even owners of larger birds complain that, to their surprise, finches are really messy. There are ways to minimize the untidiness, but I do not know any finch owner who has eradicated it completely. The good news is that most of the time the mess is confined to the cage area!

Molt can put the bird room into a shambles, with feathers flying everywhere. They molt once yearly, shedding and replacing every single feather on their body. A small hand vacuum can help, as can providing them with a bath at least once or twice a week.

Cleanliness is vital to the health of your birds and your family. Remember that finches put their little beaks on everything, so as soon as there is poop -- usually within 5 minutes of you finishing cleaning up -- they have the potential to pick up germs. Here is a general idea of how I clean my cages:

Daily: Wipe down the bars and grate with cleaner, removing all visible droppings. Replace drinkers and feeders and with clean, fresh water and food. There is nothing more important than clean water, so replace it several times daily if possible. Change the papers at the bottom of the cage.

Every week: Perches are cleaned. They are easy enough to pull out, wash or pressure-wash, and replace. Keeping 2 sets means a little less hassle.

Monthly or every few months: take the empty cage outdoors, spray with water, and scrub with cleaner or bleach. Let dry in the sun.

Where Will You Clean Cages and Accessories?

It's worth thinking about where you'll wash food and drink containers before you acquire finches. The bathroom sink? The kitchen sink? The dishwasher? Does anyone in the family have a problem with that?

I know that many people wash their bird dishes in the dishwasher; I personally wouldn't be able to eat from my dishes if I knew the birds' things had been in there! So I do not use it. Generally I clean cages outdoors where they can dry in the sun, and on the rare rainy day I wash them in a bathtub with a hand-held sprayer.

Multiple Pets

Finches do not fit into an active, multi-pet household as easily as many pets. It is easy to add a second or third dog to a family. Adding birds, a completely different species, is another thing altogether.

Finches are prey animals. Their predators include most other common pets, including cats, dogs, rats, mice, snakes, and bigger birds. Birds are essentially wild (not domesticated) animals, so their instincts remain strong. Watch a dog approach the finch cage and observe the wariness in the finches. They know to be afraid. Because of this, finches must be kept safe from all other pets. Be sure that, if you allow your finch to fly free, other animals are secured in another room. *Always.*

I hear stories time after time like this: "Our dog Spot never bothered the birds... for years he ignored them.... but we left the door open and Spot killed the birds."

The pet predators featured in the stories have been dogs of every breed, cats, and parrotlets, lovebirds, and parrots; the story remains the same. It is hard to imagine sweet Fido or Kitty killing your bird, but it can and will happen. As the guardian, you must protect your finches from predators--even your own sweet, furry ones. Be diligent. Keep finches out of reach. Do not let larger birds fly free around the finch cage without supervision. Secure cats away from the bird area at all times.

I have to tell you that, as I am doing a second edit on this book, my young parrotlet is sitting with me at the desk. He isn't very hand-tame, but he will stay on the computer or on my shoulder--usually. There's also a puppy in a 4'X4' pen. located in the middle of three open rooms totaling around 1100 square feet. Safe, right? Well, no. The bird flew directly into the 4X4 pen just now, of all the places he could have flown! Fortunately, my husband and I both ran to the rescue, and the parrotlet flipped himself around to the outside of the wires before the dog got him. Crisis barely avoided.

Most likely the bird would have bitten the dog, as this type of bird is feisty and thinks he weighs 100 pounds.

Still, it is *always* best to keep them apart, especially with finches that are primarily caged with no escape route.

Do They Fit with your Lifestyle?

Keeping any animal is a serious responsibility, but keeping birds is especially so. They are not domesticated, and you are completely responsible for their health and happiness. A bird can sit all of its life in a tiny cage being miserable, or you can offer it plenty of space and fresh food so that it has a real life.

Many people travel, and owning finches can throw a wrench into the plans. A trustworthy pet sitter is a must. Too many people rely on a family member or friend to care for their pets, only to learn that the friend let the water go dry or forgot to feed them and the birds died. So plan on hiring a professional pet sitter when you travel--one who's knowledgeable about birds. Be aware that some pet sitters are not familiar with birds, and refuse to care for them. (Hint: start looking for someone early, or you may end up staying home!)

Other people find that their family or housemates were not in complete agreement with having finches. They do not care for the mess, or they simply don't like the noise, or they smoke--which is toxic to finches.

For those with a great many house guests, the finches must be considered. During a large party, it might be easiest to simply remove the cage to a quiet room and shut the door. For smaller groups, it is possible to ask them to respect the birds. I find that there is an idiot in every group--that one person who tries to take a finch out on his finger (letting 10 out of the cage in the process), or the one who pokes at them repeatedly, or the small child who opens all the doors. Because of this, I always remove all the birds to a safe, closed location before guests arrive.

What About Family Members?

Gouldian finches are good pets for *almost* everyone--but not absolutely everyone. If family members are not on board with having birds, close the door on the bird room and they will not see, hear, or smell them. However, even the most ardent no-birds parent or spouse is usually won over by their beauty and tiny song.

Because Gouldians are small and quiet, they are considered good pets for children.

However, children must be taught to respect them. Finches do not handle stress terribly well, so excess noise and activity is a concern. Feeding unsafe items and improper handling (such as tapping on the cage or putting hands in the cage for no reason) can take its toll on a bird. People who don't have time to teach children not to open the doors, not to poke the birds, etc., probably shouldn't choose finches as pets.

On the other hand, for families that take the time to educate kids on how to care for their finches, owning them can teach responsibility and care that will carry through a lifetime. Part of this responsibility will be that children use indoor voices to protect the birds, and also that they'll educate their young visitors to do likewise. These are great leadership skills for children to learn!

Finches are great pets for single people. Being away from the home most of the day is not a problem, assuming you left them food and water. They will chirp and sing nicely (but quietly) when you come home, which most people find relaxing. They are easy to care for, which also makes them good pets for seniors.

Finches do *not* make good pets for smokers. Cigarette smoke is lethal to birds, as are candles and most air fresheners.

Many people get into the world of finches with little knowledge about how these tiny beings are actually going to change their existence. Their appearance draws us in. But actually having them makes us notice the tiniest change in body language or behavior. Outdoors, we begin to see how native birds interact with one another and react to external stimuli.

However, it is important before taking on any living thing to know the amount of time, the financial cost, and the physical labor involved in owning it. A lot of that will depend on how many finches are taken on. Let's take a look.

How Much Time I Spend On Birds Daily

This is only a run-down of my own schedule, which has varied as my numbers have gone up and back down. There are surely others who clean faster, cook more efficiently, etc. Bear in mind that some of my visit is spent talking to them or just admiring them.

When I had six finches and they lived as a colony on the screened porch, it probably took less than 30 minutes a day to change feeders, drinkers, papers, and wipe down the cage. Plus we spent hours observing them, and probably fiddled with things constantly.

At one point they lived indoors in a bird room and the numbers got up to 100; it took nearly three hours a day to clean, cook their food, and feed. I'm sure a little birdwatching was in there as well.

Right now there are about 30 birds in 9 cages, and I spend one hour in the morning changing paper and drinkers, washing the dishes, feeding dry food, and checking on all the birds. I call it my well check, which I will explain a little further on.

Later in the day I prepare cooked or chopped food and serve it on paper plates, which are easy to dispose of after a couple hours. I double check on everything done earlier - occasionally a cage was missed or a drinker has fallen off the side, or a baby is on the cage floor. So that's probably another 15 to 30 minutes.

*In the time since this was written, I have reversed the feeding schedule so that the fresh chop and sprouts go in the cage first thing in the morning when they are hungriest. A dry mix is fed around 5 pm and is safe to remain in the cage overnight.

Preparing for Your New Birds

When getting new birds, people get so excited they forget everything. Nearly every time someone visits my home to purchase finches, they've forgotten to bring a cage, for example. So here's a list to help you. It's in the Appendix as well.

Have a new cage set up before getting the birds. Place perches and newspaper inside and fill the feeders/drinkers. This will help reduce stress on them because you won't be reaching in to arrange things.

If there are already birds in the cage they'll live in, rearrange the decor, then add the new birds late in the day if possible. It seems that if they 'sleep on it,' they're more accepting of one another.

Take note of the kind of feeders and water containers the finches are accustomed to. For the first few days, provide both the old type and new type, or even just set a dish of clean water on the floor. Water needs to be easily accessible in the first days. Many birds don't see it or forget where the water source is, and they can become quite thirsty.

When picking up a new finch, there are tiny finch carrier cages that are the safest way to travel. These need to have food and water containers in them no matter how short the trip is. A regular cage or a sturdy box (with breathing holes) would also be acceptable. If using a dog crate, cover the holes with screening so they can't escape. Many people attach perches in the crate, but they are safe on the floor where they won't be jostled off a perch in the moving vehicle.

While traveling, if the vehicle is especially hot or cold (10 degrees Fahrenheit difference from the room where the bird was living) it is helpful to cool or warm the car before placing the carrier inside. Covering the carrier with a sheet helps to keep them from panicking as they ride.

Upon arrival at home with the new birds, check to be sure the cage is still secure (and they're inside it!) before opening any vehicle doors. Nothing is more upsetting than a bird escaping from the car, knowing it probably won't live more than 24 hours.

Many people wonder how to move their new birds from the travel cage into the permanent cage. If it is possible, this works well: clip open the cage doors using a clothespin or paper clip, first the permanent cage then the smaller one. Hold the travel cage door against the other cage door... and wait. Murphy's Law says the higher the cage door is, the longer you'll probably have to hold it before they decide to fly over—until your arms are aching. At least that's my experience. If another person is available, he can slip a dowel, pencil, or chopstick between the back bars of the travel cage, which might encourage the finches to fly forward.

20   TANYA LOGAN

If you want to, it is perfectly acceptable to capture the birds with your hands or a small net and transfer them to the new cage.

After placing them in the cage, leave them alone for some time; they need to rest and explore their new environment. Cover the cage on three sides with a sheet or blanket, until they become familiar with their new home.

2 | I Prefer Ranch Style With a Pool

The Gouldian Home

10 Easy Facts About Cages

1. Buy the biggest cage you can afford
2. Bar spacing should be 1/2" which is measure from the center of the bars. Bigger spacing is dangerous.
3. The simpler shapes (plain rectangles) are better
4. Brand matters; buy a quality cage
5. People have definite cage color preferences, so find out what yours is.
6. Used cages *with no rust* are acceptable if sanitized first.
7. Cage size for a pair of Gouldians should be 30X18X18 minimum.
8. Store employees generally do not know what the best size is; stores are looking for profit not birds' comfort.
9. Birds fly horizontally, so consider buying 2 cages to open side by side for better flying space/better physical health.

10. Smaller access doors are preferable so the birds cannot escape.

The most frequently asked question: I bought finches at the pet store and the employee sold me a 12x12 inch cage, is that good enough?

Answer, accompanied by a deep sigh: No. The minimum size for a pair of Gouldians should be 30X18X18. That gives them enough space to fly from side to side. Being able to fly is a key to good health.

A good cage is one that satisfies both the bird and you. By this I mean the bird has ample space for flying, a comfortable place to perch, and good feeders/waterers. Ample space for such a tiny bird is not nearly the same size or expense as if you were purchasing for a large parrot. Cages can be had for $12-$100 that are large enough for your birds.

Purchasing a cage seems like a simple exercise, but there are many 'right' and 'wrong' cages on the market and readily available. It is best to read and learn before you make an investment. The right cage should last for years.

For the Gouldian finch, space to fly is a must and that means side-to-side space. They do not fly straight up and down. Flying is essential to a finch's health; if you do not have space for a cage that allows them to fly, it is best not to purchase a Gouldian finch.

Style may matter to you because you want the cage to fit into your decor. But that's not the only definition of good style! It makes a difference to the birds because the style of cage you pick will have a lot to do with their comfort and well-being. Let's take a look at some bird cage styles.

For you, the cage needs to be pleasant to look at, easy to clean, and safe for your birds. Aesthetics, as we know, are in

Figure 2-0-1 Aviary, Author's own.

the eye of the beholder; you can find finch owners who only buy black cages, some who only buy white cages, and some who use very tiny mesh from Home Depot to build their own. More recently, it's become popular to DIY a wooden aviary from a recycled cabinet or entertainment unit. I have a gorgeous wood-and-glass aviary built by Oak Creek that I got on Craigslist for $200.

I feel that my birds show up better in white cages, and my black cages tend to show dirt more. I used to think 1/4" mesh meant you couldn't see the birds as well, but now I've changed my mind (or developed superpowers).

When cage shopping, the rule of thumb is to always purchase *the biggest cage you can afford*. More space means more room to fly, which in turn means a stronger and healthier pet.

The spacing between the bars or mesh of the cage is one of the most important considerations. For finches they must be 1/2 inch (12 mm) apart or less, but never more. More space between the bars might allow the bird's head to become trapped. This size is standard in most finch cages, so if you are purchasing from a pet store you will find many that suit you. I've also heard recently that very thin bars can bend, allowing the bird's head to become trapped even though the spacing is technically correct. These were super-cheap cages purchased overseas. Cheap cages also rust earlier than better built ones, causing a need for replacements down the line. So please shy away from the bottom-of-the barrel pricing, even though it may be tempting.

When shopping for cages, consider the ease of cleaning. Ornate cages can be more difficult to clean because of the nooks and crannies. Rounded tops are attractive but might be hard to reach on the inside. (Round cages are not good for finches because the bar spacing is irregular and can catch tiny toes or beaks. Besides, they're a waste of good flying space; finches need room to fly.) Please don't buy decorator cages or those with lots of scrollwork-- I guarantee you'll be sorry.

While shopping, take a look at the surface of the metal. Some cages are made with a stamped pattern on the surface, some are smooth with a dull finish, and some have a slick, smooth surface. The slick ones will be easier to wipe down. And of course, a powder coating is preferable to a painted surface.

If you have already perused the cage aisles in your local pet store, you know that cages tend to be tall, not wide. I do not know why manufacturers don't make what we want or need. Perhaps we don't tell them their cages are built incorrectly for our purposes.

Figure 2-0-2 Cages connected together

At any rate, many Gouldian owners solve the problem by purchasing 2 or more cages and placing them side-by-side, removing the center walls and connecting them with zip ties. This creates a doubly long cage at fairly low expense.

So how much room does a Gouldian really need? Consider that your Gouldians spend their entire life in the cage. They need to eat and drink comfortably as well as fly around. Their life will be significantly shortened without enough space to fly. So the *smallest* cage I recommend is 30 inches in length, and many people purchase the 30X18X18 model.

I debated long and hard about whether to recommend the 30X18X18 cage, because most people do not start with one pair of birds, they start with a few pairs. The moment that you think about purchasing more than just two birds, it is time to consider a bigger cage for a flock or purchase another 30X18X18 to house each pair separately. Two cages this size can be put together end-to-end. In some models this can be done by folding back one panel.

For more birds housed together, you will need more room. So, if you feel that you might purchase more pairs, go ahead and start with the biggest cage you can. Bigger cages are called "flight cages" or we often refer to them as "flights." From the 30X18X18, many people move up to a 30X18X36, or thereabout. This cage can hold about 3 pairs comfortably.

Note: There is an oft-recommended chart online that shows, in square feet, how many finches fit comfortably in a cage. Many people go by this to determine how many finches they can own for their cage size. The problem with square feet is that we are actually dealing in cubic feet--in other words, height matters. Not as much as width, but it still has a place in our calculations. I have been experimenting with cages to determine, in cubic feet, how many finches will fit together comfortably. "Comfort" refers to a cage in which the birds do not feel crowded--something that is a little hard to determine, unless you really know your birds! I have discovered that each finch pair needs approximately 6.5 cubic feet of space. This information is

- Based on my own experiments
- Only useful for Gouldians, not necessarily for other species or mixed flights
- Computed by multiplying length x height x depth, in feet.

What happens when there are too many finches in a flight? Too many can mean illness and a great deal of stress--and a lot more cleaning! They may bicker. You may see plucking or bare spots on heads, necks, and/or chests. The youngest or smallest finch becomes weak, as he or she gets pushed away from the food more than any other. There could be injuries or even 2 or 3 sudden, unexplained deaths.

One way to offset the overcrowding problem over the short term is to hang many fake plants around and across the cage. This visual break gives them breathing room from each other. Another useful item is the stress perch, where a bird can sit in his own "room" separate from others.

Can you have too few finches in a flight? No! With at least two (because they are flocking birds, so they need companionship) offer the most space you possibly can. You'll be rewarded with happy, extremely healthy birds.

Adaptability

Finches are incredibly adaptable. If the cage is moved to a new area or the flock to a different cage, it doesn't take long for these curious creatures to start checking it out, flying from perch to perch and twisting their heads this way and that to look at it. That said, an evening move keeps the stress down for some reason. Maybe by the time they've "slept on it" they feel comfortable.

Style Matters: Tips for a Better Cage

Besides size and bar spacing I'd like to share a few tips to help choose a really good cage the first time. I think we bought 3 different kinds before we found the one we like best. (see GouldianGardens.com/book_links for photos)

A slide-out tray at the bottom makes clean-up easier. Most trays are plastic these days, which makes them lightweight and easy to hose down. Some are metal; this is also quite easy to clean. Many cages feature a removable grate above the tray. Again, this is a terrific feature for clean-up because it can be carried outdoors easily and hosed off. If the grate does not come out, one must reach inside to clean it, or cover it with newspapers to keep it from getting soiled.

Another attribute to examine is the placement of doors. Do they open easily? Are they so large that birds will fly out when you open them? Doors are opened and closed often; safety is a main concern. Many cages have a "door within a door," allowing you to open the smaller one for most chores -- keeping the birds safely inside.

When the selected cage has the larger size swing-out access doors, it is possible to use a towel to keep them from escaping. I use 3 clothes pins and a dish towel to cover the opening, sliding my hand in around the towel to do whatever work I've decided to do. The birds might bump the towel by accident, but they don't go beyond it. I believe we save them from a great deal of stress by keeping them in, rather than chasing them around the house for half an hour after an escape.

What about food and water access? A seemingly small detail, yet consider that we feed two or three times daily. Many cages feature slide-up doors that to access a feeder. This is the simplest method and the least likely for bird escapes. If there are no specific feeder holes, a main door is opened to insert hanging feeders; is that door so large that birds will escape? None of these have to be deal breakers, but they are points for scrutiny, and may be more important if the birds are located outdoors or in an exceptionally large room.

Consider the material from which your cage is constructed. Nontoxic metal and plastic are acceptable; this means no zinc or brass--even the least bit will be toxic and potentially cause problems. Most pet store cages are made of acceptable material and are finished with chrome or lacquer to prevent rust. These are safe for your finch. There is no need for a play top or a top that opens because finches are not generally finger tame. When they are allowed out, they will rarely land on top of the cage.

Some of the cheaper imported cages have bars that even a finch can bend. The paint on them may flake off, leaving a rusty bar exposed. These are best avoided.

Many people have expressed their satisfaction with Vision brand cages. These are small plastic and wire cages that feature a debris guard and a deep base, which helps keep seed hulls and waste contained in the cage. I have not used them; I'm simply reporting good results from trusted friends.

Wooden cages are usually made of beech, with a drawer underneath that is also made of wood. The price of wooden cages is comparable to that of metal ones. The pressed wood tray can be replaced with a plastic or metal one for ease of cleaning. Cages made of wood can be quite beautiful. The negative of owning a wooden cage is that wood retains moisture, creating a breeding ground for bacteria and mold.

Pagoda style cages abound on the market, as do other fancy styles--townhouses, castles-- and antique cages. Consider the ease of cleaning; all those nooks and crannies make for a long cleanup detail! These are more of a decorator item than functional bird cage, and you may find yourself dumping your investment in a short time. I once owned a townhouse cage... it's gone now!

Buying Used Cages

In the past many people advised "No used cages, ever." this was because of illness, parasites, and fungi that might lurk in the corners and crevices. More recently, many are giving up that preconception in favor of finding a bargain.

If the cage can be cleaned, and it meets all the criteria listed in this section, it is acceptable to purchase a used cage. Remember that it is not possible to know, when buying a cage from a garage sale or newspaper ad, what lived--and died--inside it.

A "recycled" cage must be thoroughly washed and disinfected prior to use. This can be done by removing all perches and dishes and scrubbing the entire cage with Dawn or similar dish washing liquid in lots of hot water. Disinfect it by making a mild bleach solution (1:20) and wiping every surface thoroughly. Rinse, and allow the cage to air dry. Even better, spray it with F10, a product that is made especially for disinfecting against pet illnesses.

If there is rust present, the cage can be repainted using ECOS gloss or Rust-Oleum paint, which is bird safe (except for the metallic Rust-Oleum, which is not recommended for pets). At the time of this writing, Rustoleum Painter's Touch was certified toy-safe so it can be used for bird cages. ECOS is good too, but requires a primer when painting on bare metal. Either way, allow at least a week to let the paint not only dry, but the vapors release.

A problem several friends have encountered recently with used cages is finding nests of cockroaches in the legs of the cage. Be sure, if there are openings, that you have cleaned and disinfected in these as well! Perhaps covering them would help prevent future outbreaks.

There are some beautiful antique and vintage cages that can be found on sites like Craigslist and eBay. Antique lover that I am, I'm not able to recommend them. There are too many possible hazards. Besides the construction, what paint or lacquer has been put on it over the years? What rodents might have used it for a nest, thereby leaving droppings or other detritus behind? What finishes have been sprayed on it, and are they safe? What about pesticides? Antiques are best left for decoration only.

DIY

Building one's own cage is not difficult and can be done using a variety of materials. Many people build a 36X20X36 or larger cage for under $200 with the materials of their choice. I share these resources for the reader to get ideas; cage construction is beyond the scope of this book.

Hardware cloth, a lightweight screening material, is often suggested for construction cages. But birds are able to ingest the zinc particles on the cloth, and zinc is toxic to birds. Likewise galvanized wire, electroplated cages, and galvanized hardware such as bolts and washers all contain high levels of zinc.[i] It is possible to remove the zinc dust (the loose zinc powder) from the product by scrubbing it with vinegar. This does help with the powder and loose bits, but it does not remove the zinc layer itself.[ii] Many breeders use wire that is galvanized after weld (GAW) as a cheaper alternative. But as this wire is exposed to the elements, a white powdery coating develops – which is the breakdown of heavy metals. So birds are still at risk of exposure.

Should you be concerned about zinc? There are a couple of schools of thought on this topic. One argument is that finches do not chew on the cage wires like other birds such as hook bills. It is true that they don't chew *as much*; but you can still see them placing their beak on the cage wires from time to time.

Can zinc be removed? YES, by soaking in acid solution or sandblasting. But then the product is more apt to rust--so you'll have to paint it with a non-toxic paint. It may or may not be worth the effort. It will be left to the reader to decide. But there is no sight sadder than a bird dying from zinc toxicity. Nothing can be done except watch as it suffers through it.

Alternatives to Galvanized Wire

- PVC coated wire has a thin layer of plastic over the wire. Since finches and softbills are not big chewers, this is a safe choice for cages.
- Stainless steel mesh does not rust, is non-toxic and is available at most hardware stores.
- Powder coated wire is more expensive than PVC coated but the coating is baked on, making it sturdy and long-lasting.
- Wood is safe if it is labeled untreated. Use the wood as a frame and staple mesh on the sides, top and bottom with a staple gun.

When building a cage, be sure to select a type of construction that will hold perches. Quarter-inch mesh, for example, will not have room for the typical perches that have a single slit on each end for sliding over the bar, so there will have to be some other method of mounting them.

For further reference, there is an excellent cage-building guide on efinch.com, several how-to videos on YouTube.com, and a terrific DIY aviary group on Facebook.

Indoor Cages

Before purchasing a cage, it is best to decide where to put it--and not just for aesthetic reasons. Never underestimate the importance of thinking through your cage placement. It literally means life or death to your birds. They need to be safe from predators, heat, drafts, and toxins. There are pros and cons to both indoor and outdoor cage placement. For example, now that I have birds indoors, I can no longer use my favorite plug-in scents, perfume, or hair spray; they are toxic to birds. It is certainly not a deal breaker, but it is a consideration, especially if the whole family is not on board with owning delicate birds. Here are a few more indoor dangers:

- Cleaners (including vinegar, which is a safe cleaner but the fumes are toxic at full strength), bleach, and ammonia
- Incense
- Candles
- Plug-in scents
- Spray scents, perfume, deodorant
- Smoke of any kind including cigarette, , marijuana, cigar and pipe smoke
- New carpet or paint
- Round metal Protective Mite Killers that hang on

THE GOULDIAN FINCH HANDBOOK   33

the side of a bird's cage

- Teflon or PTFE coatings on pots & pans, self-cleaning ovens, clothes dryers, new hair dryers, space heaters, irons, waffle irons, deep fryers, heat lamps.[iii]
- Clear glass – they try to fly through it and can break their neck – one of mine flew across the lanai (screen cage) and crashed into the glass, landing motionless on her back. I'd just witnessed someone giving mouth-to-mouth to a bird the week before, so I picked her up and blew on her face. She began breathing and within a half hour was back to normal.
- Holes in screens, or loose screens. Obviously a small finch can escape easily or be injured by loose wires; repair these as quickly as possible, and install all screens securely.
- Water – I've had babies drown in little more than 1 inch of water. Finches must have a very shallow bowl for bathing. If allowed to fly free, water in toilets, bathtubs, and spas should be off limits.
- Toxic foods: chocolate of any kind, alcohol, avocado, garlic, onion, salt, yeast-risen raw dough, and coffee. Any beverage with caffeine. Spoiled food. Fruit or vegetables with possible insecticide residue on them.

Gouldians can be made nervous by regular household activity, so they need to be somewhat out of the way of traffic--say, in a corner of the family room. It is also important to consider the source of water in relation to the place you'll be washing bird dishes. Is it nearby?

The kitchen area is the most dangerous for any bird, especially finches due to their small size. Toxic fumes from

Teflon coated cookware has led to the death of many pet birds, so out it goes. Anything that is burned in the kitchen may give off toxic fumes. So can a brand-new oven, an oven's self-clean cycle, and silicone baking mats. By the time an owner realizes what is happening, it's usually too late. Best to place the birds away from the kitchen.

Airflow and lighting are the other two concerns for cage placement. Finches need air circulation for health, but must not be in the way of drafts (like in front of an external door). They need light, but having a cage in direct sunlight may cause them to overheat indoors. Instead, place them out of direct sunlight, and utilize a full-spectrum light that helps their bodies utilize much-needed UV rays.

As prey animals, finches feel unsafe sitting out in the middle of a room or looking out a window where cats or predatory birds are in view. A few thoughts about cage placement:

- Windows can be a source of stress
- Higher is better than low, especially if 4-legged pets are present
- Hallways or entryways are too busy
- Kitchens contain more toxins than any other room
- Bathrooms are too humid
- Away from vents, heaters, A/C units
- May need cover at night to prevent disturbances and/or drafts

With indoor cages, a lot of problems can be solved by using curtains, shower curtains, or fabric panels. Finches feel safer with at least some cover, so you will usually place the back of the cage against the wall. But then there are the droppings they fling on the wall...so tack an inexpensive shower curtain behind the cage for easy washing (and less repainting). If the cage is located such that there is space behind it, clip some fabric or cardboard onto the back to make the Gouldians feel secure. The cover can extend over one or both sides for even more security. This is especially useful with new birds, or when the cage is moved and they seem stressed.

Covering cages at night is not strictly necessary, but shadows, insects, and rodents can cause "night frights" -- when the birds fling themselves from one side to the other, hitting cage sides and anything else in their paths. One solution is to cover the cage at night using a light cloth. The other choice is to use a nightlight, so there's less change due to cloud cover, storms, or shadows.

Cages Outdoors

Keeping birds outdoors is more common in other countries than here in the USA. Most of that is due to our weather, which can be extreme. Gouldians originate from an area where the weather is fairly dry most times of the year, and where temperatures range from 70-95 degrees Fahrenheit. Therefore, they should be acclimated to or protected from temperatures outside of that norm.

To keep caged finches outside, it might be reasonable to consider using 3/8" mesh around them instead of the 1/2" bars. Doors will need to be secured, too, in order to prevent entry by predators or young children.

All outdoor finches require some sort of shelter they can get into that will protect them from the elements -- wind, rain, snow, and bright sunlight. This can be as simple as a wooden box with a small entry hole on one side.

Read on for some issues encountered when keeping finches outdoors.

Snakes - I once approached my outdoor cages, stood on tip-toe to check on a breeding cage, and realized I was eye-to-eye with a snake! He'd eaten three of the four babies in the cage, which made him too fat to get out. This snake squeezed through ½" bars.

Rats and mice are at least as bad as snakes, and they seem to find endless ways to get in. Oftentimes owners can't determine how they've gotten access. In addition to physically harming the birds, they carry many parasites and illnesses. If at all possible, keep rodents out of the food, water, and aviary.

Hawks, falcons, and owls are a constant threat in many areas. They are able to enter the top of screened areas and are quite aggressive if hungry.

Foxes, badgers, squirrels, weasels, mink -- the list goes on. Humane trapping or a call to pest control is often necessary.

Keeping Birds in an Aviary

Technically, the definition of an aviary is an enclosure that is tall enough to walk into. Many people refer to their larger cages as aviaries. With finches, it doesn't take much to create a large spacious enclosure-- so it is easy to fudge on the description.

Anyway, an aviary affords your pets a large living space. It may contain plants or shrubbery, which is as attractive to look at as it is useful. Many aviaries are built by the owner (DIY) but there are commercial ones available to fit all lifestyles, budgets, and sizes. Frames are built of wood, PVC, or metal. Some aviaries are built on the ground or on a concrete base; others are suspended to keep them off the ground.

The thought behind an aviary (besides the fact that you can have more birds!) is that birds breed best in a large, natural environment as opposed to a cage. Before deciding to build one, ask yourself if you are a more hands-on or hands-off owner. If you like to watch them and are content to let nature take its course, you would probably be happy with an aviary. If you prefer to select the pairs, peek into the nest, raise babies by hand and so forth, you might prefer using cages.

When building an aviary, there are many considerations as to materials. Depending on the environment, it may need to be heated or cooled. If the sides are entirely created from mesh, then there'll need to be some sort of enclosure inside the aviary where the birds can gather for warmth or shelter. On the other hand, if there is an enclosure, you may need to plan for ventilation.

Another good safety measure for an aviary is to create a protected entry. This can be as simple as a second screened-in doorway. You enter, shut the first door, then open the second door. If a bird does escape in your direction, he's trapped in the enclosed entryway, where you can catch him fairly easily.

Due to predators many people build the aviary with two layers of netting or mesh for walls, allowing some inches in between. This makes it doubly hard for the predator to get in. Since some hunters can enter by digging underneath, countless aviary owners set it on a concrete pad with heavy skirting around the bottom of the wall. Even so, this requires frequent inspection to be sure nothing has breached the fortress. Others bury the lower end of the fencing and pour concrete over it to hold it down.

Disease and parasites can be carried into an aviary by rodents, cockroaches, and even ants. We've already discussed how to keep rodents out. Insects can be prevented by using diatomaceous earth in or around the aviary. It is safe for birds and other pets, but will kill insects.

Wild birds may harbor internal parasites that can be passed on if they roost or nest nearby. These parasites are treated through a protocol discussed in chapter 9, Illnesses and Treatments.

A Few More Cage Accoutrements

Gouldian finches do not go crazy for baths the way society finches do, but it is still an integral part of finch keeping. Baths can help them through molt, and can cool them when they are stressed or overheated. For those involved in shows, baths help keep feathers in pristine condition. Plus -- they enjoy bathing! You can also take advantage of the bath, adding a product like KD cleanser to the water to repel insects and mites, as well as killing germs. When it is time to treat with S-76, this too can be added to the bath water. Birds that are used to taking baths will eagerly self-medicate, saving you the trouble.

There are bird baths made especially for cages, which you can see on the website, but you can provide a shallow dish or tray from around the house. Rectangular plastic carryout trays from oriental restaurants work quite well, as they are free, easy to clean, and six birds can bathe at once (but if you have 15 birds in the cage, they will all do their best to join in!).

There are two important things to remember when offering a bath. One of them is that the water absolutely must be shallow. If it is more than 1/2" inch deep, your bird or baby birds could drown in it. I remember my very first non-green fledgling came out from the nest, a cute yellow one, and within about an hour of fledging, had drowned in the water dish--which I thought was quite shallow!

The second thing to remember is to keep the water absolutely clean at all times. That is because finches make a habit of taking a drink from their bathwater. I usually put in baths in the morning, while I'm setting out fresh food, and remove them within a couple of hours. By then everyone who intended to bathe has done so.

Cage Floor

Many cages come with grates in the bottom, which may or may not be removable. Most people find that they prefer to be able to remove it, even just for ease of cleaning. We pull them all out and pressure wash them, which is quick and simple. Some bird keepers feel that grates are hard on birds' feet and may cause injury, especially to young fledglings, so they remove the grate permanently. Taking the grate out does eliminate one step of cleaning, but if the owner is not diligent the birds will end up eating their droppings thereby possibly ingesting germs or parasites.

Thinking about the grate placement, or lack thereof usually leads to this question: What do I put on the cage floor?

With the grate in place, the cheapest substrate by far is newspaper. Simply spread it on the tray beneath the cage and remove daily. It can be stacked in 7 layers so that one layer per day is removed. It can also be placed on top of the grate, which we do whenever babies are present to help keep them from falling between the grate bars if they should fall from the nest.

Some people prefer a printless paper and purchase big rolls of white paper at stores like Sam's or Costco. The paper can be cut to exactly fit the cage tray. This can be a relief if one cannot bear the sight of the few inches of newspapers that occasionally drape out over the cage tray; I'm way too lazy for that.

I recently read a rumor that the print on newspapers was deadly to pet birds. This is an unfounded story; in the US, newspaper inks have been plant based for many years. By the year 2000, 90 percent of daily newspapers were using soy-based inks. So newspaper is safe, just not as aesthetically pleasing.[1]

End rolls of newsprint are sometimes available at a local newspaper office.

Other options are reclaimed pulp waste, like Carefresh Small Animal Bedding, on which the packaging states *"This short fiber pulp is free of ink, dye, clay and other chemicals that can be used in the paper making process."* Using this is good for the environment and healthy for the birds.

It is best not to use corn cob bedding because of its tendency to attract mold and bacteria. One should also avoid pine shavings, as the oils are toxic. This is due to their composition; the oil is structured with monoterpene hydrocarbons.

Aspen shavings are available in bulk at most pet stores and are nontoxic. They make a safe, gentle bed for fledglings learning to fly, and are perfectly safe if they nibble on them. The advantage of aspen is that it stays in place a tiny bit better than some other shavings -- although it still can be messy.

One type of bedding I experimented with in some cage trays is horse stall pellets, officially called "Equine Pellets." They're relatively inexpensive and have no excess odor. Friends who swear by them spread them in the cage trays and can leave them two or three weeks, with a little raking in between. When soiled, they can be removed with a shop vac. They do not become dislodged like the shavings do, and they make the cage look quite attractive.

I had four unexplained deaths in a row, with the only link being that those two cages both had the equine pellets in the trays. I removed them and have not used them since. Some months later, I read that sawdust (which is essentially what these compressed pellets are) can off-gas ammonia. That may explain the problem, especially since my enclosed bird room is fairly small. The friends who are successful with them keep their birds in a larger area. This is only a guess and a personal experience -- it will be left to the reader to decide. I cannot recommend them.

Temperatures

I get many inquiries as to whether birds are too hot or too cold in this temperature or that. Gouldians hale from a tropical climate, so they can *generally* withstand hotter temperatures than most birds. That said, your birds and mine probably didn't really come from a tropical background, right? Perhaps they were hatched in somebody's very temperate 70-degree living room. The temperature our birds can withstand have more to do with recent generations than their origins, I would say.

The rule of thumb is that they need to remain within 10 degrees of their "normal" temperature in order to be comfortable. Some people go to great lengths to maintain this. That's for people who feel their birds are delicate; I feel they are wildlife and are hardy, with a few caveats. So here is my answer to the temperature question.

In general, Gouldian finches are safe down to 50 degrees Fahrenheit and up to about 85. BUT there are many variables to be considered within that range. On the cooler range, is the wind blowing, causing a wind chill of many degrees lower than the absolute temperature? Do they have shelter? Is it raining?

On the hotter side, is this the first day of hot weather? Are they in the sun, with no shade available? Is it extremely humid? What's the heat index?

Gouldians that are going to be kept outdoors where temperatures are above 85 degrees need access to shade and possibly an automatic sprinkler or fans to cool them. When the weather is hot and also very humid, they are more apt to become ill (and food will spoil quicker). If purchasing Gouldians to keep outdoors in the heat, try to buy them during the spring months so that they can acclimate gradually.

Gouldians that are going to be exposed to colder temperatures -- below 50 degrees-- need shelter and a heat source. One can find many breeders who will say that theirs are kept at much colder temperatures without harm; however, until the birds have built up their tolerance, it is best not to chance it. Outdoor aviaries may be rolled indoors, or a "room" can be constructed from wood that will allow them to retire to their own indoor box complete with a thermostat-controlled heater. This box will need several locations for eating and drinking.

If it's cold and the birds are fluffed up, they are trying to retain heat. Infrared heat bulbs, heat panels that mount on the wall, and thermal perches are a few of the heater types one might use. There are also aviary-specific heaters with a fan and filter. I like oil-filled radiators for an efficient heating system that will hold a consistent temperature.

Humidity considerations

Because Gouldian finches come from a subtropical climate, they and their eggs need a constant humidity of 50 to 70%. For areas where this level is not normally met, owners can simply spritz the room with a fine mist of water a few times a day, or supply baths. The Gouldians will get the humidity they need by taking a bath and then when they sit on the eggs supply the moisture that they need as well.

Lighting Considerations

Spend a little time online reading about finch keeping, and you will no doubt learn that birds need UV rays because of vitamin D3 and calcium. But most reports are more than a little muddy about the specifics, and many are misinformed about which type of lighting provides the right sort of spectrum. There are few studies on the effects of lighting to bird health, but you may hear "the number one best thing you can do for your bird is provide good lighting."

Here's exactly how vitamin D, lighting, and metabolism interact.

Our birds have a preening gland, called the uropygial gland, located right above the base of their tails. You may have noticed that they touch their beaks to this area when they are preening. That's because the gland produces oil, which birds spread over their feathers.

The oil contains a compound 'precursor D' (7-dehydrocholesterol) that, upon exposure to UV rays, produces vitamin D^2. So we could say a bird creates the vitamin D by spreading the oil around. The next time he preens, he gets some of the vitamin D in his beak and swallows it. His digestive system will then take the vitamin D and convert it to D3.

The other part of a bird's metabolism relates to his eyes. A bird's eye absorbs red, blue, and green spectrums like ours, but also can absorb UVA and UVB rays. That's why their vision is so good, and why they can find food easily that we can't even see. Take away the UVA, and it's like making them colorblind.

Furthermore, the UV absorption interacts with his endocrine system to regulate migration, day/night, and molting patterns. So you can see that lighting is not just about calcium absorption, but about the entire health of the bird.

If finches are kept in outdoor aviaries, they receive enough sunlight to promote the creation of vitamin D3, which in turn helps them to utilize calcium and all the other important bodily functions. The problem arises when we *don't* keep them outdoors. Inside, even if they are near a window chances are the owner keeps that window closed the majority of the time. Window glass usually contains a barrier that filters out the sun's rays, the very rays birds need in order to synthesize vitamins. So for bird health it becomes necessary to use lighting that simulates sunlight -- although if you can get them outside for even a half hour a day, sunlight is always best.

Before delving into the specifics of lighting fixtures, let's remember a couple of definitions from high school biology:

A <u>Kelvin</u> is a measure of light's color.

<u>Spectrum</u> is the wavelengths of energy produced by a light source, measured in nanometers. The human eye can see from 380 to 780 nm.

The best bulb for avian use is referred to as a full-spectrum light (not one that is labeled simulates sunlight).

You may have read about the color rendering index, or CRI. That is a scale telling how close an artificial light is to natural sunlight at noon. With noon's light value given the number 100, lights are scaled accordingly. So we don't ever see an artificial light with a score of 100 but we can find many with a CRI of 94-96, which is quite acceptable for our purposes.

THE GOULDIAN FINCH HANDBOOK   45

Much has been written, repeated, and misconstrued about the use of fluorescent lighting with birds. The controversy began because of cheap, older fluorescent fixtures that had a flicker of about 60 cycles per second. They're hardly worth mentioning now, but because it's still out there on the Internet let's discuss them._

It is not the tube, but the light fixture that causes flicker. There are several ways around this problem. The first is to increase line voltage frequency, through the use of higher quality ballasts - say, an electronic ballast rather than the cheaper magnetic type ballast. The electronic ballasts are more energy efficient, as well, saving the user money on electric bills. In fact, purchasing a good high-quality fixture and using a decent T8 bulb in it will increase your light-hours, thereby offsetting the extra expense for the fixture itself.

Many bird owners are also fish or reptile owners, and perhaps already own special lighting. These lights are similar, but not ideal for birds. Fish tank lights have blue-range UV spectrum, which is not the one we want. Strong reptile lights can burn birds' retinas, rendering them blind or nearly so. Lighting for birds can be bird-specific or found at the hardware store.

An example of good lighting would be 200-watt Compressed Fluorescent Clear White lights rated at 2700K or higher. These can be found at a local hardware store. Another nice option is a miniature cage light made by FeatherBrite, which I'll link from the web page*. At $80 at the time of this writing and 15 watts, it is an excellent value for our purposes.

One concern is that the UVB portion of a light bulb starts to disintegrate soon after putting a bulb into use. I stumbled on something while contacting ZooMed regarding their CFL bulb. Here's what they told me via email:

The glass of the bulb is made from special UVB transmitting quartz glass for maximum UVB penetration, however it is the special phosphorous coating on the inside of the bulb that creates the UVB as the light goes through the glass. Without this coating it would not be able to emit the UVB rays. The Kelvin rating for the bulb is 6800K.

So perhaps the ZooMed bulb produces UVB over a longer period of time than some other bulbs.

It is a good idea to mix bulb types, if there is space and the budget for several. This way light levels can be raised or lowered by using more than one bulb. Also the light will be spread more, giving all birds an opportunity to sit close to a bulb. The birds will appreciate some form of shade alongside the lights; we use artificial plants but one could use live plants, small trees, hanging feeders, or even carefully placed dollar-store Frisbees.

Let's see why mixing lights might be necessary. Say a breeder uses a fluorescent tube fixture, laying it directly on top of the cage. This is a popular choice because it is an easy, safe and convenient way to provide lighting. It also puts the light fixture 18 inches from the perch, which is the recommended amount.

Now suppose the birds in this cage only roost on the top perch at night, but spend most of the day at mid-cage on their boings and tree limbs. The amount of light they are getting has been greatly reduced. By installing smaller clip-on lights at the side of the cage, one can re-introduce full spectrum lighting for healthier birds.

The manufacturer will make a recommendation for the distance from the cage to place the light, and it is important to carefully follow this recommendation.

A timer will help regulate day/night cycles. Birds may have up to 15 hours of daylight without harm to them or their reproductive system.

For safety reasons light bulbs and cords need to be covered or at least inaccessible to the birds. If there are uncovered light bulbs in the home or aviary and birds fly free, they could get burned.

At night, birds appreciate and even need a night-light if there is no ambient lighting. That is because finches are prone to night frights, similar to humans having panic attacks or night terrors; they become frightened of something, real or imagined, and flutter frantically and violently about the cage. This often will injure a bird. He literally can beat himself to death, or become stuck in the cage bars. Having a night-light helps him to calm back down.

If you overhear a night fright happening, you can enter the room and turn on lights, speaking gently to your birds. This will help them to settle more quickly, but don't be surprised if they continue to thrash for a few moments after you've come in.

Web page: Please visit http://www.GouldianGardens. com/book_links . You can find all links mentioned here, as well as updates to this issue of the handbook.

Cleaning the Logan Way

Cleaners don't disinfect, and disinfectants don't always clean. There are as many ways to clean a bird cage or bird room as there are owners! Here I will outline my way, which hopefully will contribute useful ideas to the reader.

Daily: Wipe down the bars and grate with cleaner. This could be a mixture of vinegar/ water, a few drops of lemon oil in water, a bleach wipe, or Poop-Off spray. If there is a buildup, it's easier to spritz the droppings with water first, let it set for ten minutes, then proceed with cleaning using a scrubbing pad.

Remove drinkers and feeders and replace with clean, fresh water and food. There is nothing more important than clean water, so replace it several times daily if possible. Bacteria grows in water fastest of all, followed by fresh foods that are left sitting out.

My feeders and drinkers are hand washed in a big laundry tub using Dawn dishwashing liquid. I rinse them, refill the sink, and add bleach to the water, soaking for 10 minutes. This is because bleach cannot disinfect properly if the dishes are dirty; they must be clean before they can be sanitized. Be sure to rinse thoroughly after the bleach wash; we take an extra measure of allowing the dishes to dry for a day or so before re-using them, so that any bleach that may remain will dissipate.

Many people wash their bird dishes in the dishwasher; I personally wouldn't be able to eat from my dishes if I knew the birds' things had been in there. So I do not use it. The dishwasher does clean and sanitize thoroughly – it is acceptable to everyone else, just not me.

Every few days: I use F10, a product used by many veterinarian's offices, which according to their literature is "effective at recommended concentrations against all types of bacteria, fungi and spores including MRSA, avian influenza, psittacine beak and feather disease, canine parvovirus, E.coli, aspergillus and a host of others." (https://www.f10products.co.uk/f10-sc-veterinary-disinfectant-product-information/) I wipe grates and bars with it. This product is expensive, but it is a concentrate so it lasts a long time.

Weekly: Perches are sanitized. They're easily scrubbed/ bleached and hosed off. Keeping 2 sets means a little less hassle.

Wearing rubber gloves and surgical masks while cleaning cages and accessories is a good practice because some illnesses birds carry are zoonotic, meaning they can be passed to humans. The mask ensures that any dust in the air won't be inhaled.

It isn't that finches are especially dirty or even that we've encountered any of these illnesses, but rather that every step taken to prevent illness matters -- for humans as well as our finches.

Table 1 Clean and Sanitize

Product	How to Use / Dilution	Must rinse?	Leave on time	Useful For
Dishwashing liquid	as usual	X	--	General cleaning
Poop-off	Spray on/ wipe off		--	General cleaning
Chlorhexadine	3 oz. to 1 gallon	X	10 min.	Kills salmonella, some viruses, yeast
Bleach	1:10	X	15 min.	Kills Mycobacterium, Polyoma virus, Giardia, Borna virus.
Vinegar	1:3	X	30 min.	General cleaning
F10	1:250 4 ml to 1 l; for stronger strains 1:100 (10 ml to 1 l)			Kills bacteria, fungi, most viruses Circovirus and Parvo

| Ammonia | 5% | X | 45 minutes | Kills crypto-sporidium and coccidia |
| Virkon-S | 2% | | 10 min | Kills PBFD, Asper, myco-plasma, avian influenza, hundreds of others |

iv

3 Where Shall We Put the TV? - Cage Accessories

Accessorizing a finch cage is fun. Look online and you'll see plenty of ideas, some better than others. I like to see cages lined with artificial turf, but I don't believe I could keep those clean enough for my flock. What I can do to decorate the cage is hang fake plants all around inside and out, so I'm content with that.

Nests are one item people tend to buy almost immediately. I've never bought a finch from a store, but I imagine store personnel must encourage this thinking. So the buyer comes home with one or more nests. There are a few reasons I'd like to discourage this.

- It's best not to breed new-to-you finches. They need to be treated for parasites and vet checked, even if they aren't ill (and some are). They could be too young.
- Birds do not need a nest for sleeping. They can sleep on a perch. So people who don't plan to breed them don't need a nest.
- Gouldians *can* use those little wicker nests you see at the big box stores, but they prefer a deeper box type nest. Remember, they're cavity breeders. So

something that feels like a dark hole in a tree will suit them best.

The problem with the wicker nests is that they're quite deep and yet not very wide. So for more than 3 babies it's crowded. As the babies grow the space issue becomes worse.

One way to resolve this is to fasten the nest at an angle up to and including 90 degrees so that the babies are using one of the long sides as the base of the nest. This gives them plenty of space, and the parents don't mind the door being strangely angled.

Wicker nests should be disinfected after use, as should plastic ones. Wicker nests are not easy to clean thoroughly, and they aren't really made for re-use.

The plastic boxes for nesting are ideal, as they are easy to clean and the birds seem to know right away what to do with them. Many people suggest the deeper nest is better; all I know is most of my birds like the type that is wider rather than long.

Specifics about nests are addressed more in the breeding chapter.

Perches and Accessories

Because our bird spends most of his life on his feet and on a perch, we must give a great deal of thought to the materials our perches are made from. He needs surfaces for standing and balancing as well as movement.

When purchasing a cage, one probably will receive a perch or two with it in the form of pine dowels. In my experience they are always too big --the diameter should be such that the birds' toes will wrap about 3/4 of the way around. Much as you don't wear the same shoes every day, their little feet need to grip various surfaces to keep from developing sores, and to keep up the muscles in their feet and legs. And using the same surface day after day can wear callouses on their feet. So it is recommended to use several different kinds of perches in the cage.

Perches may be made of concrete, wood, rope, or plastic. The plastic ones are easiest to clean and are *least* favorable to little finch feet. Concrete or sand coated are good choices because the nails receive a natural "trim" while using it. However, never use the separate sandpaper covers for a perch -- they will damage your baby's feet. Also these are not the ideal surface for the finch to stand on all the time.

There are nice perches made from wood branches, which come outfitted with a wingnut and screw so they fasten onto the cage. These are also easy to DIY. Or, if you have trees available that you can identify as non-toxic and that have not been sprayed with chemicals, it is perfectly acceptable to put a branch into the cage, propping it at the angle you please or sliding it through the cage bars to suspend as a perch. This offers surfaces and angles for gripping and climbing. Leave the bark on, as it helps with foot health. When the branch is too dirty to use any more, it can be thrown out and replaced.

The negative of wooden perches, both natural and dowel, is that they grow bacteria easily, because they are absorbent. They must be cleaned and rinsed thoroughly at least twice per month, and maybe even weekly.

Birds also enjoy simple ropes, like cotton rope or rope toys. A tight twist in the rope will ensure that nails do not get snagged on it. If you see a bit of the rope fraying, simply cut it off with scissors. Rope perches can be tossed in the washing machine monthly and hung to dry. They

Figure 3-0-1 Rope Perch © Cornel Volschenk

must dry completely before being replaced in the cage.

Whichever type of perch you select, consider buying twice as many as needed so you have some for using while you wash and dry the other set. Perches needn't be placed in the bottom half of the cage, as most Gouldians do not perch there. Put them at the top and place two or more far apart from each other. Perches placed at the ends of a cage encourage flight across the length of it. We always want to encourage as much flight as possible.

One of my current set-ups has small dowel perches placed at an angle in the upper back corners of each cage. Just below that, I've put the longest tree branches my cages will handle. I just stick them through the bars so the feel fairly stable, and clip off the excess with pruning shears. I have a pile of cut branches on the back porch so I can grab one when there's a branch that needs replacing. That's because we only have palm trees, so I have to beg branches from others who have 'real' trees when they trim. I notice that the birds choose the branch perches over the dowels every time. I don't currently have the concrete style purchase in my cages, and it shows in the long growth of their nails, which means more work for me.

*Some of the concrete style perches shipped from overseas have recently been found to be built on a lead-based core. Several parrots have died from them. It is not as dangerous to finches as hookbills because finches do not generally destroy their perches, so the core would not be exposed. You may choose to avoid them anyway, just in case.

Cups, Bowls, and Baths

Bowls and feeders may be made from plastic, stainless steel, ceramic, or even glass. You will find yourself straying away from bird-specific items in favor of something that works. One item I like to use is tiny glass votive candle holders. They are perfect for serving up eggshell or minerals, and the finches seem to like them. I get mine at the dollar store 3 for $1 and throw away the candle. I also have found tiny ceramic feed dishes at Pier One and Michael's. Get creative -- you can use almost anything as a feeder. Egg cups, decorative wooden troughs, Chinese take-out trays, and vintage dishes are all useful as bird feeders. So are bird feeders that are normally hung outdoors for wild birds to use.

Many people use an inverted mason jar similar to a chicken feeder. Set that contraption in a shallow clay planter tray, and the seeds that are tossed will remain inside the tray. I prefer a higher feeder. Or maybe because my husband does all the vacuuming, I don't really care about the mess...

The general rule is that plastic dishes scratch and can retain bacteria. I use quite a few plastic feeders myself; they're cheap and they hang nicely on the cage bars. Yes they scratch, and I deal with bacteria by soaking them in bleach every time I wash them.

This is another area where you'll want to have at least two sets of dishes on hand. That way one set is in use and the other has been washed, disinfected, and is drying.

Most finch owners provide one feeder or trough for seeds, one for pellets, another for fresh food, and another for eggshell or supplements. Add to that some will be in the wash, and you see that 4-6 containers of some sort per cage are needed.

Waterers

Water is of the utmost importance because of their health. Birds are messy, and they'll deposit food, droppings and feathers into their water. As soon as a dropping enters the water, the birds run the risk of a nasty disease that can spread throughout the entire flock. Plus they often put seed in their water, soiling it further. For these reasons, the open watering trays that come with the 30 x 18 popular cage are not a favorite of bird owners. Even with a cover over them, the water can become soiled quickly.

Some people like to use tube-style waterers. I personally am not a fan of the ones they lick (like you give to rabbits and guinea pigs) because I hear too often about them stopping up, and if the owner doesn't notice the animal dies. I use the drinkers that are a tubular shape, but have a small drinking tray that protrudes out from the bottle. You can find the link on the Gouldian Gardens website. Birds adapt to this type of waterer fine, and it keeps the mess out of the water for the most part. This type of bottle can also be used for seed or supplements.

Note: Be sure to give them the type of drinker they're accustomed to along with the new one for a few days, or until you know they've learned to use it.

Toys

Finches are said not to like toys, and they don't play with them in the way bigger birds do. That said, they will usually utilize swings, cotton ropes, boings, and other things they can land on. I can't say enough about swings. They love them. Some enjoy preening toys. Many like toys they can shred or pull apart, things with fringe, bits of fabric, etc. A basket of hay will keep them occupied for hours. Finches enjoy baths, so a container large enough to hold an inch of water is a favorite.

Things That Make Life Easier

Finches are excessively messy, so there are cage additions that will help keep things clean. These include:

Cage guards or Cage bloomers. These can be purchased, or home made from fabric or plastic. place the guard around the lower 6 inches or so all the way around. This helps to keep the seeds and hulls inside the cage.

No-mess birdfeeders. These are sometimes referred to as seed corrals. They're created in a way that seeds are not flung everywhere.

If breeding, a clean container for nesting material will allow them to build their own nest – a feed bowl, plant saucer, etc.

Water supply close at hand. This goes back to where you are locating the cage - the closer to a water supply, the better!

A grate cleaner. This tool scrubs droppings off perches better than anything else I've used.

On the website, you'll find photos and links to these items, as well as any others I might have discovered since writing this book. https://gouldiangardens.com/book_links

4 I Eat Like a Bird - Feeding the Lady Gouldian

Ten Tips to Feed the Best Diet Possible

1. Variety is key to obtain the best nutrients
2. Buy the best you can afford
3. Make food available at all times
4. Avoid all-anything diets: all seed, all pellet, all fresh foods
5. If they are not accustomed to pellets or fresh food, introduce slowly
6. Expect some food waste
7. Finches only eat about 1/2 teaspoon a day
8. The best nutrition comes from fresh vegetables and grains
9. Cleanliness is a must! Clean dishes, wash produce, etc.
10. Never stop improving their diet.

Gone are the days of feeding strictly seed to birds -- and purchasing that seed at the local department store! Through research, it has been found that birds need a variety of foods in order to be healthy and live long, productive lives. These days birds are fed pellets, seeds, sprouts, and fresh fruits and vegetables. It is a testament to this better understanding of nutrition that they now can live much longer than the oft-quoted "average" lifespan.

Seeds and Nuts

If you have Gouldians on a seed-only diet. There may be baldness, especially in egg-laying hens. They may have a scruffy appearance or shortened lifespan when compared to your friends' Gouldians. They may lay fewer eggs than average or raise only one to two offspring at a time. All these are signs of dietary deficiencies.

Consider the diet in nature. In the wild, we would observe that they eat seeds, mostly from grasses, and part of the year they'd also find berries, insects, and other treats. Because we have many options available, it is easy to provide our finches with sound nutrition. Let's start with seed mix.

Finches need seed. There is a vast array of seed blends on the market. They can be purchased at big box pet stores, bird-specific stores, feed mills, health food stores, and online. You can even mix your own. The best seed mix will contain several types of seed; most owners have to experiment to find which ones their birds are willing to eat. They tend to toss the ones they don't like to get at the ones they prefer.

Many mixes are "fortified," meaning they contain added vitamins and minerals. Some people argue that the additives are useless because our finches remove the seed hull before eating the inside. Others feel the seed manufacturer knows best, and has conducted research to provide the best nutrition possible. If the owner does not select fortified seed *and doesn't provide other foods* it will be necessary to supplement with vitamins (see the supplements section at the end of this chapter).

What about those mixes that contain vegetables, pellets, and seeds? One veterinarian says, "Unfortunately, the vitamins and minerals are impregnated into the seed hulls, which are discarded when the bird eats the seed. Often pellets, dried fruits and nuts are also included. The pellets are often rejected by the bird, in favor of the seeds in the mix. As nutritious as the pellets may be, they do the bird no good on the cage floor."[v]

The basis for a seed mix normally consists of some various millets and canary seed. Canary seed is produced by the canary grass, *Phalaris canariensis*. White proso millet is a favorite of most finches, followed by panicum, Japanese and red proso millet. Niger seeds are high in protein but also high in fat. They can be used, but they're best restricted to the colder parts of the year, when finches expend more energy to keep warm.* They are also beneficial to hens prior to breeding. Other seeds often included in a mix are German millet, red Siberian millet, and rape seed.

There are many choices, and several 'levels' of seed mixes. A more reputable company may have a higher quality mix, and they may take measures to ensure their products do not contain moths or beetles. Seed can also be obtained at most bird markets, although if they are not carefully packaged they may be exposed to germs or insect infestation.

Owners with a substantial number of finches often find a supplier they like and purchase seeds wholesale. Others go a step further, purchasing individual seeds and mixing their own special combinations. Some even supply each type of seed separately in a dish, so the birds can pick out what they want.

If you wish to try mixing your own seed from scratch, here is a recipe is from the Finch Society of Australia (FSA)[vi]:

20% plain canary seed
30% red panicum
15% white millet
10% panorama millet
10% Japanese millet
15% yellow panicum and/or Siberian millet

The authors of *Grassfinches in Australia* recommend this mixture: 2 parts red panicum, 1 part canary seed, and 1 part Japanese millet.[vii] The book notes that red panicum is softer and digests more easily than the others. On page 24 he breaks down the nutrient content of various seeds. Two points stand out. One, the protein content of these three seeds is about 13-14%, while that of Niger and rape seed is over 20%. Secondly, by feeding only these seeds and no other foods the calcium: phosphorus ratio, which ideally should be kept at 2:1, is skewed wildly.

*None of my birds have ever willingly eaten Niger seed.

Protecting Seed from Moths, Grain Beetles

Occasionally, seed mixes are contaminated with moth or beetle larvae. These are generally not dangerous to the aviary, but they are annoying and often difficult to eradicate. Keeping seed in the kitchen means inevitably one will find them raiding the flour, other pet food, and much more. Therefore prevention is key. To do so:

Transfer all new feed to an airtight container and store it in the refrigerator or freezer. Freezing for 7 days is said to destroy the cycle.

Keep all enclosures extremely clean, with no old seed or hulls laying around.

Another alternative is to mix some diatomaceous earth into the seed bag. DE is a product made to kill beetles, fleas, and other crawling insects. It is safe for birds, and may help deworm them in the process. Here in Florida indoor bugs are almost a given, so I sprinkle a tiny bit of DE in the trays below the cages, too. I have not had a problem with insects, except for a couple bags of 'discount' seed I purchased at a bird mart. In trying to save a few dollars, I wasted a lot more. I threw that seed away along with most of the contents of my kitchen pantry, and purchased a chest freezer where I now store all bird food. Lesson learned!

If you do notice beetles or moths, do not use spray pesticide; instead, clean all cages thoroughly, inspect your seed and toss any product that looks contaminated. If moths are present in a cupboard or cabinet, remove all items, storing boxed goods like crackers or cereal in the refrigerator or discard them altogether. Vacuum every surface where the bugs could have been present, especially corners of the walls where the cocoons reside. Be sure to discard the vacuum bag you have used. Continue this practice at least every 10 days until there are no signs of live moths, beetles or larvae. It feels like it takes forever but this too shall pass.

Some owners use sticky fly strips behind the bird cages and shelves where moths or beetles have been. Many birds become stuck on the strip or rip out feathers trying to escape it. For that reason I do not recommend them.

Spray Millet

Spray millet is a favorite treat and many breeders make it available at all times. It is especially useful for juvenile and just-weaning Gouldians. Spray millet contains protein and carbohydrates, and is rich in potassium, phosphorus, and niacin.[viii] It is fairly low in fat, and because it can be clipped to the cage-top they can forage in a manner similar to wild Gouldians--it's good exercise. There are many styles of millet holders available, from hanging styles to tray-like devices that hang on the side of a cage, or simply use a heavy binder clip to suspend it from the top of the cage. Gouldians love hanging onto the stalk to eat the seeds. Have fun experimenting to see what you and your birds prefer.

I currently provide one millet stalk to a smaller cage or two stalks for six or more birds, once weekly. For fledglings, soak it up to 1/2 hour first or until chitted.

Spray millet is messy because they throw the hulls. I highly recommend thinking about its placement in the cage. Hanging it in the very center keeps more of the hulls inside the cage. Hanging it lower would probably do so too, but they love to have it at the top.

Hemp -- a Secret Superfood?

Hemp seeds aren't mentioned much, at least in my circles, but they're sometimes considered the king of finch foods. They contain a complete amino acid profile, whereas most seeds, beans, and legumes are incomplete. They contain trace minerals, several of which our finches tend to lack. They have the highest amount of protein present in any plant, anywhere. They even have omega 3 and omega 6 fatty acids. Consider adding hemp to your regular feeding regimen. Other healthy seeds are chia and flax seeds. Buy the ground variety of all these seeds if you can find them. Most finches can't break through the hull of hemp seeds, in particular.

Sunflower and Safflower Seeds

There's always a lot of comparison between safflower and sunflower seeds. Both of them have similar nutrition, with safflower a little more expensive and apparently not as good-tasting. Finches cannot hull these seeds, so these seeds are served shelled and chopped or ground. Either seed in moderation is good. There's probably no benefit to using safflower over sunflower seed. Both seeds are fatty, so unless you are trying to supply fatty foods on purpose (never a good idea with caged birds) it's best not to feed them too much. Another reason to avoid high-fat diets is possibly limiting calcium absorption. We spend so much time trying to give our birds calcium, it doesn't make sense to take it away.

I hate to mention this old rumor that sunflower seeds were addictive. Maybe that started because cockatiels like them so much! At any rate there isn't any truth to it. Birds like them; but just as we like chocolate, there should be a limit.

What in the World is Milk Seed?

"Milk seed" is a term used mainly in Australia referring to the green stage of panicum (millet) seed heads, the stage before they ripen enough to be harvested. There is a tiny window where the green seed heads are in a milk stage, which Australian Gouldian expert Mike Fidler is reported to have said are 400 times more nutritious than dry seed[ix]. The milk seed has to be harvested and frozen within a scant half hour in order to retain these valuable nutrients.

To feed milk seed, simply serve it frozen - it doesn't even have to be thawed out.

Figure 4-0-1 Finches Eating Millet.
Photo © Tina Billings 2020.

It is so important to their diet that in the wild, the Gouldians time their breeding season to coincide with the availability of this green seed.

For those of us who don't live in Australia and don't own acres of land or fields of red and white millet, how can we provide "milk seed?"

One option is to provide sprouted seeds. (See the next section for details on sprouting.)

Sometimes products pop up that claim to provide nutrition without the trouble of soaking and sprouting. In my opinion these are corn based (possible yeast), processed foods; I have trouble seeing them as equal to fresh sprouts.

Nuts are not discussed too omuch in the find world, but they are a great source of protein. They are fatty, but they supply omega-3 and omega-6, both necessary to good health. Nuts must be shelled and ground before Gouldians will attempt to eat them; otherwise they go to waste.

Fresh Vegetables, Fruit, Sprouts, and Microgreens

Nutrition is key to any finch keeper's success, and variety will ensure great nutrition. The same superfoods that are best for humans are great for finches as well. With a small adjustment to your evening salad, you'll be able to share a portion of it with your birds. I am 'mostly' vegan, so I set aside portions of my meals on a regular basis before adding onion, garlic, or seasonings. My birds' diet has slowly moved toward more fresh foods, which I believe is great for their health and is proven by their longevity.

Even veterinarians agree that fresh foods should make up at least 25% to 80% of a bird's diet. There is little need for fruit since finches don't seem to care for it, so most of these foods will be vegetables, nuts, and grains.

In general, vegetables containing a large amount of water will have less nutritive value. An oft-repeated fallacy is that iceberg lettuce is "bad" for finches. It's not bad, as in toxic or

The Tomato Controversy

While researching for this book, I found a Veterinarian who included tomatoes on his list of acceptable foods for finches. I was surprised; normally aviculture rejects tomatoes. So I dug a little deeper. It seems that the leaves and stem of tomatoes are toxic to finches. The fruit, although not toxic, is extremely acidic. Some birds will react strongly to that acid. Because there are more nutritious fruits and vegetables available, I would say skip the tomatoes in favor of something we know to be both healthy and safe.

Figure 4-2

harmful; it's just watery and doesn't contain much nutritive value. Other types of lettuce are more useful. However, if you are trying to convert finicky finches to a fresh food diet, do consider using lettuce as part of that plan. They love to nibble it and drag it around. Just don't overdo it because watery foods can lead to watery droppings.

Some of the best health foods for finches are kale and broccoli. Some of the most-liked foods include scrambled eggs and cooked sweet potato. I live in a sub-tropical climate where it's possible to serve my birds flower blossoms and palm fruit as part of their daily diet. Even one weed that grows rampant here, purslane, is a healthy food for birds! So don't overlook your flower garden or even your back yard when considering your birds' diet.

- Raw egg
- Chocolate
- Alcohol
- Apple Seeds
- Salt
- Uncooked beans, and all Castor and black beans
- Coffee or Tea
- All raw and uncultured milk products
- Acorns
- Rhubarb

Fruits and vegetables should be washed clean of pesticides and cut or shredded into teeny beak-size pieces. I use a food processor. As with all foods, remove uneaten portions after a few hours to prevent spoilage. For multiple birds, it will be easiest to make a large amount of chop (discussed later in this chapter) and freeze it, thawing out only what you need each day.

68 TANYA LOGAN

Recommended Fruits and Vegetables

Apple	Cherries	Pear
Apricots	Bok choy	Peas, cooked & mashed
Asparagus	Coconut	Peppers of all kinds
Banana	Corn	Pineapple
Adzuki beans cooked or sprouted	Broccoli	Clover, red and white
Bean sprouts	Cucumber	Plum
Chick peas (garbanzo), cooked or sprouted	Dandelion leaves	Pomegranate
	Dates	Potato
Lentils, cooked or sprouted	Endive	Pumpkin
Green beans	Fig	Rapini
Mung beans, cooked or sprouted	Grapes	Raspberry
	Grapefruit	Brown rice, cooked
Bulgur wheat, soaked	Kale	Romaine lettuce
Beet	Kiwi	Spinach
Blueberry	Melons	Sprouted seeds
Broccoli	Mango	Squash
Brussel sprouts	Nectarines	Strawberry
Cabbage	Orange	Sweet potato, steamed
Cantaloupe	Papaya	Sprouted wheat
Endive	Lebanese cucumber	Chicory
Silverbeet	Rocket	Kale
Carrot	Parsnip	Zucchini
Carrot tops	Peaches	Oats, cooked or soaked

There are some foods that should be fed in moderation. Those include raw dark green vegetables- spinach, bok choy, and kale, for example-- which are high in oxalates and therefore will decrease calcium absorption (important if you are breeding). High levels of fruit are discouraged because of the sugar content. Large amounts of beans, grains, and pasta can result in obesity.

CHOPS and the Concept of CHOPP™

Chops are various chopped -up mixes of fresh, whole foods that we serve to our finches on a daily basis. They're easy to make, just chop up fresh foods and mix them. They provide essential nutrients that seed-only diets can't give. These recipes are simply suggestions; a chop is only limited by the imagination. Be sure to check the list at the beginning of this chapter to see what foods are safe before serving them.

If you do not have time to make chop each day, consider making a week's (or a month's) worth at a time and freeze it. For finches, it can be frozen into ice cube trays. Then simply take out a few cubes each day, thaw and serve. Another way of freezing is to fill a zip-top bag (any size – sandwich size to a gallon), press it into a flat, thin layer, and freeze. This way it's easy to break off a chunk for your birds. They also store nicely, taking up little room when stacked flat.

Human baby food could be a substitute for fresh vegetables. Canned vegetables are not recommended because of the salt content. In a pinch, use a can but rinse them well to remove some of the salt. Mixing the canned food with other fresh foods that aren't canned will help reduce the salt even further.

Soft foods like chop should be offered several times a week or (preferably) daily. Once the birds are used to eating them, vitamins and supplements can be mixed right in. Remove any uneaten food after a couple hours to prevent spoilage. One aviculturist who works long hours away from his aviary serves frozen portions in the morning, which thaw through the day. He claims he has never had a problem with food spoiling.

CHOPP™ is my own acronym that stands form Creating Healthy Options for Pet Parrots and Finches Too. I prefer to use "creating" instead of "following recipes" because CHOPP is a concept. It's not a cut-and-dried formula, although I will be sharing plenty of those in this book. Instead, with CHOPP you select from each food group and build a healthy mix. Let's take a look.

CHOPP™: Building Health Step by Step

As mentioned earlier, CHOPP (Creating Healthy Options for Pet Parrots and Finches Too) is a concept, not a formula or recipe. The more varied your CHOPP is, the healthier your bird will be. You may be wondering, "why bother with this? Just give me the recipes!"

Let me tell a story that will explain why understanding CHOPP's concept is so important. Years ago in another life I was a violin teacher. I had a student come to me with her folder of "music." She wanted me to audition by playing it for her.

As a long-time professional, I had no problem playing sheet music on any level. I placed hers on the stand – and stopped dead. This wasn't music. It had lines like a music staff, but that's where the similarity ended. There were strange symbols written on it. There were no markings telling me about the beat or note length. If I had just played it out using the location of the symbols on the staff lines, it would not have made a recognizable tune.

My student-to-be explained that her previous teacher invented this *incredibly special writing* to teach people to read music. I struggled to hide my dismay. The problem was that by creating her own system, the teacher guaranteed that the students would never read real music, nor could they leave her to study under someone else. They could only play what she translated into her music language.

In the same way, bird owners need to learn the universal language – the mechanics of CHOPP – rather than relying on recipes. Recipes are fine and can be useful when starting out, but knowing the system is better. By mastering the process, they can guarantee successful nutrition, variety, and health for their birds.[x]

Another concern I have is that people are giving "vegetables" and cutting back on pellet foods without giving protein or grains. This creates a diet that is skewed in the opposite direction from most: Instead of creating obese birds, now we are starving them. That is why I want to spend extra time discussing nutrition.

Fresh, Frozen, Freeze Dried? Oh My

There's a lot of misinformation floating around about offering frozen foods. The difficulty arises because every food freezes differently, and also because manufacturers might use varying ways of freezing a food depending on its attributes. For example, blanching then freezing reduces water-soluble antioxidants by 30% for peas and 50% for spinach.[xi] By contrast, one article showed "in two-thirds of cases, frozen foods had higher levels of antioxidant-type compounds, including vitamin C, polyphenols, anthocyanins, lutein and beta carotene on day three of storage."[xii] So in general *most* frozen vegetables probably are not any less viable than fresh. It is safe to use frozen foods; just check the labels to be sure the package only contains vegetables, with no added salt or sugar.

What about freeze dried? What about room drying, microwave drying, or other methods? I'm just going to summarize the many National Institute of Health articles I've read, which determined that for most foods, the best drying process is either drying produce at room temperature or freeze drying. These processes do not reduce most nutritional value and in some cases actually increase it. In studying these articles I only looked at foods for human consumption that pet birds can also eat. In other words, I skipped over items like coffee beans, which have no place in the avian diet.[xiii]

Creating Healthy Options for Pet Parrots
and Finches, too!

In general, fresh is always best. But because of storage, the small amount our birds eat compared to the size of food packaging, and the fact that we're combining many foods together – freeze dried foods and frozen foods are useful and safe.

To work from the CHOPP principle, choose the largest amount of food in your mix from the largest area of the pyramid– the bottom. That's the dark leafy greens section. The next largest amount of foods will come from the yellow and orange (and red) section and so on. When you get to the top, fruit and seed mix are about 15% of the diet, with herbs and oils being even less. More herbs are fine, but using more oils means providing more fat – something we don't want to do.

Note that sprouts are not shown in the pyramid. That's because sprouts are from every part of the chart – they're greens, yellow and orange, seeds, grains, and so on. So sprouts are each type of food, and should be included in the diet in large amounts. I do not add them to the CHOPP mix that I make as a big batch and freeze, instead I provide them fresh *with* the mix each day. That's just a personal preference; it's fine to freeze sprouts.

The list of vegetables is not exhaustive. It should give you a start. The amounts listed are merely a suggestion for a starting chop. As long as the amounts vary in pyramid style (more from dark greens, less from grains, a little oil) the mix should be healthy and well-balanced.

Dark Green Vegetables - Choose 3 or more

Beet greens
Bok Choy
Broccoli
Brussel Sprouts
Cabbage
Collard greens
Cucumber
Dandelion Leaves/Flower
Endive
Kale

Mustard greens
Peppers (green and hot)
Peas
Rapini
Romaine lettuce
Spinach
Swiss Chard
Watercress
Zucchini

Red/Orange/Yellow & Root Veg Choose 3 or more

Beets
Carrot
Corn
Parsnip
Pumpkin

Red, Yellow Peppers
Sweet Potato
Tomato
Turnip
Winter squash

Fruit Pick one

Apple
Apricots
Blackberries
Blueberry
Banana
Cantaloupe
Cherries (not the pit)
Dates
Fig
Grapes
Grapefruit
Kiwi
Melons

Mango
Nectarines
Orange
Papaya
Peaches
Pear
Persimmons
Pineapple
Plum
Pomegranate
Raspberry
Strawberry

Herbs pick 1 or 2+

Basil
Coriander
Ceylon cinnamon
Cloves
Dandelion leaf
Dill
Ginger root
Holy basil
Horseradish root

Lemongrass
Marjoram
Mint
Parsley
Rosemary
Star anise
Thyme
Turmeric root

Grains Pick 1 or 2+

Amaranth
Barley
Kamut
rice (brown)

Quinoa
Oat groats
Teff
Wheat

Protein Choose 1-2

Dried insects (mealworms, arbica fly powder, mixed)
Eggs, boiled

Seeds/ Nuts Choose several

Chia
Flax
Hemp
Millet, Any Type
Pumpkin
Sesame
Hazelnuts
Pecans
Almonds
Walnuts
Pepitas

Sprouted seeds *(see Sprouts section)* - *As many as possible*

Oils – add only 1 TBSP per 2-4 cups.

*Oils should not be overdone as they will cause the appeal of CHOPP to be lost.

Castor
Coconut
Palm

Other

Leaf Lettuce
Coconut flakes,
unsweetened
Flower petals (edible
flowers only)
Rose hips, crushed
Avian Teas
Freeze dried vegetables
Dried vegetable powder

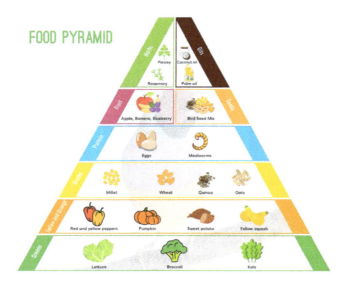

Figure 4-0-2 Food Pyramid.

The foods shown on the graphic are just reminders; anything that is in the category counts, unless it's on the unsafe list.

A few frequently asked questions:

Are frozen foods acceptable? Yes. They are nearly as good as using fresh foods.

Are sprouts healthy? Sprouts and microgreens are healthier than the seed they come from. Don't be afraid to use lots of sprouts.

Can I use the food processor? Yes – just don't run the processor until the food is pureed. Starting with the hardest foods (like whole nuts) and move to the next. Save eggs for last and barely chop them, otherwise they turn to a glue-like mess.

For a larger flock, consider buying a separate freezer for storing bird food. We did this, and it's made a world of difference. Storing seed kills off moths and beetles, and storing CHOPP keeps us from having to make it so often.

Protein Foods

Egg is one of the simplest and most commonly offered sources of protein. A cup of boiled, chopped egg contains 17 grams of protein. Other options are mealworms, bloodworms, and packaged insects. Some breeders argue that Gouldians don't eat insects, and it is true that they may not seem interested if they're unfamiliar. Offering insects during breeding season often works, as does mixing the worms with honey or other sweet foods. I provide them by mixing freeze dried mealworms and crickets with their chop. Chop is like magic at our house; we hide many things in there.

Because finches need extra protein during breeding and molting, it can be given to them in the form of egg food. The Internet contains tons of recipes for egg food; there are also some in the Recipes section of this book and in my previous book, *Feeding Finches*. Providing egg food can be as simple as scrambling or boiling an egg or as complicated as adding fresh eggs to a variety of chopped vegetables and vitamin powders. You can get as precise and complicated as you want; you can also create your own mix. You can cook it fresh or make big batches and freeze them.

In addition, there are many dry commercial egg food mixes available which provide the extra protein needed. These are especially handy for owners who work away from home and cannot remove fresh foods through the day. Egg food mixes are usually made by baking a flour-based 'bread' with high egg content, then crumbling it into finch-size nuggets. Sometimes the protein ingredient is dairy products instead of eggs, and since finches cannot digest dairy it is important to read labels.

These egg foods are considered a supplemental food, not a major food source. If you're planning to use one, do your homework and study the sugar, wheat, preservatives, and artificial ingredients. It is not worth using if there is too much junk food in it, because you can easily make your own fresh egg food.

I keep both fresh and high-quality dry commercial egg food on hand and feed both. For the finicky or newer members of the flock, I mix commercial dry egg food with my fresh blend so that it creates a crumble; they seem to like it on the dry side. Later, they learn to like the wet food too -- so I can serve my homemade egg food alone, or even fresh veggies without adding dry egg food.

Sprouts

As a seed grows into a young sprout it magically transforms into a super food. Sprouted seeds are a favorite of Gouldians, and they provide nutrition in the form of protein, vitamins, and minerals. They are lower in fat than their unsprouted counterparts. Sprouts are especially useful for young chicks and for birds in molt. If you want healthy birds - sprout!

Getting started sprouting is easy, as it only requires some seeds, a glass jar with a piece of cheesecloth to cover the top, or even a kitchen colander. There are sieve-type lids made especially for screwing onto wide mouth jars, and if you want to get really fancy, you can purchase a tiered sprouter online. There's a link to the one I use on at GouldianGardens.com/book_links.

The seeds used for sprouting must be somewhat fresh; even the sprouting mixes sold at the pet store alongside the bird seed may not germinate. Many bird owners simply gather the uneaten seeds from their bird cages and sprout them. One easy way to find sprouting seeds and beans is to visit the local health food store, where they are generally available in bulk. They are also easy to find on the Internet. Over the years I have been sprouting, this practice has become more popular and it's fairly simple to find "bird mixes" for sprouting.

Sometimes people only rinse seeds the first time, not as recommended. Their seeds will not sprout. When I explain they have to be rinsed through the process, they often that is too difficult and they won't be providing sprouts to their Gouldians. I felt deeply sorry for these birds, often originally mine. They are accustomed to eating sprouts and not only love them, but leave my home in great health. If these people tried sprouting a few times, they'd see that it gets easier and faster with time.

How to Soak Seeds

A dry seed is dormant, and by soaking it you change its makeup from a seed to a plant. While soaking, it will fill with water so lots of water is required.

Prior to soaking seeds, some people clean them by culling the ones that are broken or 'look different.' I do not bother with this; the pieces will rinse out of the mix as the process takes place.

In sprouting pre-mixed seeds of several varieties, some types of seeds will take longer than others to germinate; that is OK. The early sprouts will just grow a slightly longer tail while waiting on the slow ones. If you prefer, you can purchase individual portions of each type and sprout them separately. I've made a sprouting chart for reference. This is also available as a PDF at www. GouldianGardens/book_links

Soak and Sprout Times for Various Seeds, Nuts

Soak 0-7 hours

	Soak	Max Sprout Time
•Walnuts	4	(no sprout)
•Pecans	4	(no sprout)
•Wheat	7	3 days
•Barley	7	2 days
•Kamut	7	3 days
•Quinoa	2	2 days
•Rice	5	5 days
•Pepita	6	2 days
•Sunflower	2	3 days
•Teff	3	24 hr.

Soak 8-12 hours

	Soak	Max Sprout Time
•Almonds	8	12 hr.
•Lentils	8	12 hr.
•Millet	8	3 days
•Fenugreek	8	5 days
•Sesame	8	2 days
•Poppy	8	2 days
•Spelt	8	3 days
•Rye	8	3 days
•Garbanzo	12	12 hr.
•Peas	12	3 days

Other

- Mung 24 hr.

No Soak

- Hemp
- Flax
- Chia
- Brazilnut
- Alfalfa*

—*Although many sources list alfalfa sprouts as safe, there's one form which isn't -- the dormant seed, which contains toxic L-canavanine[xiv]. Provide alfalfa in powder form instead.

Sometimes instead of sprouting, people want to soften the seed it so it's regurgitated easily by adults and digested easier by the young. It can be soaked for 8 hours, or in a time crunch boil the seeds for 30 minutes. They must be thoroughly cooled after boiling. It is also possible to "soak" seeds by microwaving the seeds and water for 10 minutes, then rinse and microwave again for 3 minutes. This type of soak in itself does not add nutritional value; just makes it easier to eat.

Two Ways to Sprout Seeds

Mike Fidler has researched Gouldians in Australia for over 30 years. Here is his method of soaking: Place 2.2 pounds of seed mix into 1 quart of water. Add 1/3 tsp of Virkon-S and 1.25 quarts water. Stir, then soak for 2 hours. Drain but don't rinse, let set closed for 12 hours then remove lid. Sprout for 14 to 30 hours. These sprouts will safely freeze up to 1 year. Mr. Fidler also has sprouting videos online.[xv]

The following is my own way of sprouting seeds, which is a bit different from Mr. Fidler's.

Most seeds need to soak 2-24 hours before they will sprout. To begin a soak, rinse the seeds in their sprouter or a colander until the water runs clear. Do not under any circumstances use bleach on the seeds you plan to feed to your finches. The health food community feels that this is necessary to make sprouts "safe." Not only is bleach toxic, but it also destroys the nutrients--the reason you were serving sprouts in the first place!

Don't overdo it; seeds full of water will be much bigger than dry seeds. For a small number of finches you will be making 1/8 or 1/4 cup--or eating a lot of them yourself.

As soon as the seeds are rinsed, cover them with water. Add a bird-safe cleanser: KD cleanser, Virkon-S, Apple Cider Vinegar (ACV), or Grape Seed extract. I am currently using Grape Seed Extract. Soak for 15 minutes. Rinse thoroughly and return to the soaking container.

Add at least double the amount of water as seeds, up to five times as much. You cannot overdo the water in this step; the goal is to allow the seeds to absorb as much water as they can. Let the seeds soak overnight.

Dump the soaking water and fill it up one more time. This is my extra little step that helps prevent mold: Add the bird-safe cleanser. Only a few drops are necessary. Let it sit in that for about fifteen minutes, then rinse well. Rinse a minimum of two or three times daily over the next few days with fresh, clean water -- the more often the better. With each rinse, put the seeds back into the colander or sprouter and be sure there is good air circulation in the area they are occupying. You'll have fresh sprouts in as little as one to three days, depending on the type of seed you are using. Soak with cleanser for 15 minutes one last time, then flush with lots of water.

Birds especially enjoy sprouts when they are chitted, or just sprouted, before the tail has grown more than 1-2 mm (1/10 inch), and this is the correct time to feed them because seeds contain the most nutrition at the chitted stage. Store the seeds in the refrigerator as soon as they sprout. And of course, remove uneaten sprouts from your cages after a couple of hours.

Why seeds mold during sprout

Sometimes people give up on sprouting seeds because they experience mold growth. You can smell the change; it goes from a fresh grass scent to, well, a moldy food smell. If your sprouts have ruined, do not feed them to your bird. Even if you only suspect they have turned bad, it is best to toss them.

Mold can occur for one of several reasons:

- Seeds are not fresh
- Sprouter is not sterile to start
- The sprouting method does not include rinsing, or not enough rinsing, or not enough water in the rinse
- Humidity is high
- The seeds are not drained thoroughly between rinses (the most common problem)
- The seeds are placed in a cabinet or other area with no air movement

If you have experienced moldy sprouts, I urge you to try again, troubleshooting each of the above points. Also try rinsing with cool to cold water, and rinse at least one more time per day than you did in the past. Sprouting is fun and healthy; it's worth a second or even third try.

Deter mold by

- Providing good air circulation (don't keep the sprouts in the cabinet)
- Rinsing thoroughly and OFTEN and draining properly, every time
- Using a bird-safe cleanser in the water

Microgreens

Many people use the terms microgreens and sprouts interchangeably, but they are not the same. Sprouts are grown entirely with water, while microgreens are cultivated in soil. When harvesting, the whole sprout is eaten (including the seed) but microgreens are snipped off above the soil level.

Microgreens provide a great deal of nutrients. They contain 4 to 40 times as much nutrients as the corresponding vegetable does. In other words, a radish microgreen has 40 times the nutrients of a radish. Microgreen seeds can be purchased online and grown at home. In my area there are even sellers who will grow your microgreens for $5 a jar.

There is no discernible difference between the benefits of microgreens and sprouts for finches. Try both. Hopefully they'll like at least one version.

Pellets and Bread

Note: At the time of this writing, pellets are a highly controversial topic. Experts differ on the opinion of whether to use some, all, or none. Part of the problem is that "pellets" can run the gamut from a corn-based product that is full of additives to a highly nutritious finch-specific preservative-free product. Even the size and texture vary; some are too large for small finch beaks (although clearly labeled "finch") and some appear to be too hard for them to swallow. Here I'll try to present all sides to the discussion, before exposing my own practices and opinion.

Veterinarians for the most part encourage feeding 20% up to 80% pellet food. Many are now recommending 100% pellet food, and no seeds. On the other end of the spectrum, there are some nutrition experts who are encouraging an all-fresh food diet. With fresh, whole foods (which include seeds and nuts), they say, there is no need for manufactured pellet food.

Here's how the pellet craze began. Some years ago, researchers noticed that when finches eat seed mixes, they tend to pick out one or two of their favorite seeds and ignore the rest. Furthermore, seed mixes from some pet stores tend to contain high percentages of carbohydrates, just like the human processed foods in the grocery store. So the scientists developed pellet diets to help to meet all of a finch's nutritional requirements. Pellets have been created in different formulations that address the needs of varied life stages. They come in many shapes, flavors, and colors. Most are baked, compressed, and highly processed.

Because seeds are mainly a source of carbohydrates, which they don't need so much of, and we are constantly searching for ways to provide protein, I believe pellets do have a place in the finch diet. I do not agree that they should make up over 50% of the diet though. To me, pellets are well balanced and healthy, and a good base, if (and only if) offered as *part* of the diet along with seeds, nuts, grains fruits, vegetables, and egg food.

The most recent argument I heard on the PRO side (for pellets) is that "veterinarians feel that owners won't provide a well-balanced diet to their birds."

I'm speechless.

That's like a pediatrician saying you need to provide your children with frozen TV dinners throughout their school years because you won't ever have time to feed them properly. First, how does he know? And secondly, how in the world is an over-processed packaged food-like material better than what the parent could provide?

I feel strongly that there is no such thing as a one-size-fits-all bird food. Nutritional needs cannot be met solely on the basis of an "average, " commercially pre-pared solution in a bag, no matter how advertisers spin it. I do not see a way to judge the integrity of the foodstuffs inside the pellet, so we are dependent on manufacturers for our birds' health if we use them. We're also trusting that the bag hasn't sat in some warehouse exposed to extreme heat or cold that would alter the nutritional value of the food. Plus, if we consider the history of our human diets, processed foods are the ones we should avoid--so why would we force them on our finches? Think about bread, for example. If you were forced to change your diet over to bread only.... How would you look and feel? After a time, don't you think your body would begin to crave an apple, or a salad? Perhaps a steak?

That said, I did use a small amount of pellets, perhaps 20%, when I began writing this book. I made them constantly available, and therein lies the convenience. Kept dry, they last a little longer in the aviary than fresh foods.

Another statement with regard to pellets that's been cropping up lately is that if the bag says "complete," one should not provide vitamins or minerals outside the pellets. Now that makes sense, but only to a point - and here's why. (For simplicity's sake, let's assume that vitamins only come from pellets or additives, not from the other foods for a moment.)

First, I have only met one person out of the many bird owners I know who actually feeds 100% pellets. Most people combine various feeding methods. So that pelleted food only gives your birds a complete diet if you are the one person feeding 100% pellets and no other food.

If you are feeding, say, 20% pellets, then you are only providing 20% of the vitamins and minerals that are listed on the bag. Even if your birds' diet contains 80% pellets, they are still missing out on 20% of the nutrients needed. So where will they get the other 20%? I feel that we must supplement with vitamins even if they are only missing 20%. Otherwise, the pelleted food is in essence causing a deficiency - and that's just wrong.

Now I know the question that's coming next is something like, "But I feed kale (spinach, carrots whatever), so isn't he getting all the Vitamin A he needs?"

The correct way to really determine that is to figure out how much kale your bird eats, how often he eats it, how much Vitamin A is in a leaf of kale, how much he needs, and do the math. That makes me tired just thinking about it. Plus there are days that the pushier birds get more than the laid-back birds, or they just ate fresh millet so they have less kale. Or they just don't eat when you serve it. The whole thing gets really complicated. My suggestion is to provide some vitamins at least some of the time. That way you are covered. We talk about vitamins and other supplements later in this chapter.

Some brands of pellets seem more difficult for finches to eat than others, even though they are available in a crumble size. To keep shopping till you find one they will eat is not very economical, especially if you have only a few birds. Some companies will send samples, but there are three ways I have found to get around this and convince them to eat it anyway:

- Moisten the pellets by soaking in water, apple juice, or other fruit juice for 1/2 hour before feeding. I prefer water, as the fruit juices encourage spoilage.
- Grind them in the Nutribullet or food processor until they are smaller.
- Soak and blend them with other foods such as boiled eggs, or in chop. For me this is the easiest approach.

Dry Mix for Those Not Using Pellet Foods

If you've read my blog, you know I'm not a fan of pellet-based diets. To me, it's like offering dry bread 24/7/365. There's surely something more to eat! Besides, processed food were introduced to the American diet in the 60s, and look where that got us. I feel that if anyone ever gets around to studying the effect of pellet foods on birds, they will find a host of problems.

Instead of pellet food, I provide all my birds with a dry mix for nighttime that was created by Dr. Jason Crean at Collaborating for Avian Wellness (C4AW.org). It is fresh, smells delicious, and best of all is easy to mix. I buy one huge box and split it between my entire flock, finches to Pionus. This mix does include TOPS pellets along with many other ingredients.

Birdie Bread

If you spend any time in online in forums, you've come across the suggestion to make Birdie Bread for your finches. Bread is more useful for the bigger parrots, but it does appeal to some finches. My Gouldians were not interested, so I introduced some society finches--societies will eat anything. In no time, they had the Gouldians picking at the Birdie bread. You can fill it with healthful things like eggs, vegetables, pellets, and liquid vitamins. For those reasons, it is worth trying to get your finches to eat it.

If you find they simply do not like it, crumble the bread up and mix in a generous amount of dry egg food. Offer it on a plate so that they can pick through it. Keep offering it day after day; eventually you will find they are eating it. After they're used to the taste, you can reduce or eliminate the amount of commercial egg food you use in the mix.

If this does not work, try mixing the crumbled bread with fresh sprouts or chop. Recipes for Birdie Bread are located in the Recipes section.

Insects, Grit, and 'Other"

Insects

Do wild Gouldians eat insects? Yes, they do--especially when they are breeding. Insects provide a valuable source of protein. If you choose to supply insects to your birds, you can choose from live, frozen, or freeze dried. Several reputable online sources carry a couple of insect mixes that are apparently delicious (sorry, I don't speak from personal experience) and easy to serve in small cups. Live mealworms and king mealworms are said to be a favorite, along with maggots. Those can be raised at home or purchased at pet stores. Some veterinarians feel that mealworms are difficult on the digestive system, and they suggest limiting the supply.

If you do not care to provide insects as your protein source, you can offer boiled or scrambled eggs instead. Live insects aren't essential; they simply provide entertainment and add protein to the diet. Dried mealworms are readily available; soaking them before feeding may make them more palatable. Wet or dry, this is another food that can be hidden in the daily chop.

Here's a breakdown of some of the more popular live foods. Instructions for raising them yourself are beyond the scope of this book, but I've provided that information on the website.

Bloodworms have a high nutritional value. They are 65% protein -- pretty high for any live food. They contain iron. They thrive in still water, like ponds or abandoned fish aquariums. They can be purchased at bait shops or from aquarium fish suppliers. They come live, freeze dried, and frozen. You can also raise them yourself if you're into that sort of thing.

Mealworms contain about 20- 25% protein live, and providers of dried ones say they are 53% protein.[xvi] If exposed to sunlight, they can help provide some of that all-important vitamin D. When grown, they develop into the Mealworm beetles, a black common-looking beetle. When purchasing live mealworms from the pet shop, the larger variety MAY have been treated so they will not become beetles. The smaller ones will morph within a month or two.

Live Mealworms are taken eagerly and are easily propagated at home. I won't be demonstrating.

Termites What a great way to dispose of pesky termites! Birds like to eat them, and they're 21% protein. Termites are easy to raise and they multiply fast. They can be harvested all year around. It is said that even an ailing bird will become alert at the sign of termites for food.

One drawback to raising termites is the reaction of the neighbors. No one looks fondly on them. Perhaps this is best done in relative secret.

Some say it is difficult to find the queen, as in the subterranean species she may be 10-15 feet below ground. However, if you capture some termites from a colony and establish them in a new location, they will eventually produce their own queen and begin the cycle.

Maggots are 16% protein. They are often cheaper than mealworms, or free if you can find them. The main drawback to maggots is that they sometimes carry salmonella. It seems that this can be avoided by growing your own supply. Instructions are on the website.

The Gravel/grit Dilemma

Feed your birds grit at all times. Never feed your birds grit. That's the advice you get - so do you or don't you?

The answer is it depends on what is meant by "grit." I believe this is where the confusion lies. The insoluble kind, grit (singular) like gravel or sandstone, is **not** necessary for any seed-consuming bird that hulls its seeds before swallowing them. Pigeons and doves, for example, need this grit to aid in digesting whole, intact seeds. They do not hull their seeds like finches do. The hulls of the seeds prevent digestive enzymes from getting through, so grit helps to grind away the outer shell, making the insides available to jut digestive enzymes.

Finches hull their seeds. That's why they are so messy! So they don't need stones in their diet. In fact, this can be harmful if the grit collects in the crop, causing impaction. What finches *do* need is the soluble, organic grit like oyster shell, because it provides calcium which they need in large quantities.

Many people provide a grit mix (grits, plural, meaning minerals). This mix will contain some parts of:

- Oyster shell
- Charcoal (in small amounts, as charcoal can affect the absorption of vitamins A, B2 and K, resulting in deficiencies.)
- Sea salt
- Rock salt
- limestone
- Cuttlebone shaved into the mix
- Egg shells (microwaved first to kill germs, and finely ground so there are no sharp edges if feeding young)

There is also a need for a mineral mix or mineral block supplement, which can be purchased commercially.

As finches hull their seeds, they gulp down the whole, intact seed. So perhaps the grit they use helps to grind up these seeds. When performing a home-style necropsy I always find at least some grit in the gizzard. So it must be useful, or they would not eat it at all.

Notes:

- Depending on its source, some grit can cause heavy metal toxicity. One way to avoid this is by rotating brands or types of grits in your aviary.
- Charcoal from timber fires contains toxins, so use a human-grade charcoal available at the health food store.
- Some sources suggest washing all cuttlefish and shell grit to remove organisms
- One can also add calcium carbonate, kelp, liquid iodine, sulfur, or other trace mineral and vitamin solutions.

Vitamins and Supplements

Pet birds are notorious for having diseases that result from dietary deficiencies. Vitamins A and D3 are the immediate ones that come to mind; the calcium-to-phosphorus ratio is another. On the other end of the spectrum we see many obese finches, which brings with it another host of health problems.

Many so-called recommended diets can fool us. Even a diet of 50% pellets and 50% seeds is likely to be deficient in vitamin A, for example. Because of this, every bird owner should have vitamin and mineral supplements on hand and supply them on some regular basis. This is where each individual has to determine his or her own process, as the quantity of supplements needed will be based on the amount already present in the diet. Over-supplementation can be just as dangerous as vitamin deficiencies. Let me explain.

All vitamin compounds recommend administering once per day, but on the other end of the spectrum we have experts like Dr. Jason Crean who uses whole, raw food diets and no vitamins at all. Most bird owners fall somewhere in between the two; a daily supplement is too much but none at all results in deficiency. Some people suggest that a multi-vitamin be given every other day as a sort of compromise.

Because we feed ours a lot of fresh vegetables, we only supplement once weekly. If our vet ever finds deficiencies, we will change our process. This is where it's up to you to be part scientist and determine the correct dosage for your flock.

Besides vitamins, finches need minerals and amino acids in order to be healthy and breed well. Some multi-vitamins offer an all-in-one approach and others contain only the vitamins, with the intent that the consumer will also purchase the mineral/amino acid complex. Check labels to be sure. We give a calcium supplement in the water once a week, but eggshells, cuttle bone, and other sources of calcium are provided throughout the week along with the vast array of fresh foods as well as fortified pellet food.

There are a few supplements that are offered only during molt, or only during the breeding cycle, so some people wonder if they are worth it. I believe they are; the body changes and has differing needs at these times, and supplying the extra minerals all year around would result in over-supplementation. We provide a mineral-based supplement during molt, extra calcium during breeding, and a few specialty additions at other times, like extra B-vitamins to hens and their chicks around weaning time.

The important part of supplementation is to be aware of what finches need and how they can get it. Obtaining vitamins and minerals through whole, natural foods is always best, but not always easy or even possible; therefore, supplements are part of a complete diet.

My favorite supplement mix for Gouldians consists of the following:

> 1/2 box pet store grit (oyster shell)
> Shaved cuttlebone (perhaps 1/2 cup)
> 1-2 T dried kelp
> 1-2 T F-vite
> 1 T E-powder
> Mix well. Store in airtight container.

I'm Thirsty

Dairy Products

Birds cannot digest milk. Parent birds regurgitate food like seed and vegetables to feed their babies in the nest – not milk. When you hear about "crop milk" those birds actually are feeding cells and secretions from their own bodies which is not a milk product at all.

We mammals have a digestive enzyme called lactase that helps us to digest milk sugar. Birds don't have that, so they will develop diarrhea when fed lactose in large amounts. Since it isn't necessary nor helpful for Gouldians, it's best to leave dairy products out of the diet and give your birds their calcium some other way.

Water Problems

Poor quality water is often a culprit when one loses birds from time to time and there's no other clear answer. It's always a good idea to have your water professionally analyzed, particularly if you're having problems or suspect you might with its quality. The local health department can do this. Compounds like sulfur that give odors to tap water are usually not dangerous, although they may discourage the bird from drinking much of it. But if bacteria counts are elevated in the water supply, it's a good idea to serve spring water from a bottle to your birds.

Finches love to have a bowl of water around for drinking, and they usually bathe in it too, but if they manage to contaminate the water with feces you may see an outbreak of bacterial infection. An alternative is a bottle. My concern as mentioned before is that the ball will stick and the water supply will be blocked – and no one will notice. This can lead to the death of the bird in very few hours. Instead I use sort of a halfway solution between the bottle drinker and an open dish. My birds drink from bottles with a spout. They rarely contaminate the water, the drinkers are easier to scrub and replace, and I don't have to worry that the bottle won't work properly. I do place open dishes in the cages occasionally for bathing (more on that later).

Seasons: Utilizing an Austerity Diet

Over the past 20 years or so, many people have turned to mimicking nature by way of diet. They feel this creates the most 'natural' life cycle. In Australia, the native home of Gouldian finches, diet is controlled by the seasons, rain, and temperature. There is an austerity period where little food is available, followed by a rise in temperature and a wet season that produces seeds and insects. The abundance of foodstuffs during the wet season brings on the breeding season in finches. Therefore people keeping Gouldians in captivity are restricting their finch diet for a couple of months, then providing a nutrient-rich diet in hopes of bringing on the breeding season. It also has the advantage of preparing all the Gouldians at the same time, so that the entire aviary is on the same schedule.

To mimic the austerity season, one would reduce feeding to a basic seed mix and no green food or supplements. This would coincide with the time at which you would separate the males from females for a resting period.

Once it is breeding season, the birds are paired and the green foods, egg food or insects, and other nutrients are slowly increased. One breeder said practicing this seasonal change was the best decision he had made for his aviary.

Putting it All Together

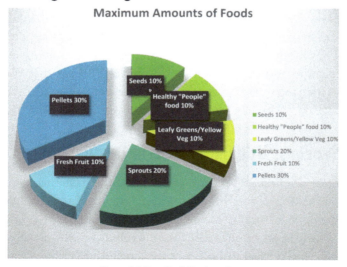

Figure 4-3 How Much Food per Day

Keep a Routine

The best way to ensure your finches get all the right foods is by having a daily routine. Finches have two times they eat with gusto, one early in the morning and one toward evening time. In a perfect world, that's when we would feed them.

Mine know that they get fresh foods in the mornings, around 9 a.m. I chose morning because they tend to eat more in the morning, and I want them to eat the fresh food quickly so it won't spoil. I would serve it earlier, but it doesn't work for my schedule. This is just what works for me; the point is to have a routine, not to copy mine exactly. I find that by always serving certain food at the same time of day, they eat it better. Others may experience different results.

By always serving fresh food, I can vary the fruit or vegetables. I don't want them to eat the exact same foods every day, but I do want them to eat what I give them. Once they've dived into the chop, they will bite into the apple, banana, red pepper, or whatever else is new in the dish. Usually they'll eat it.

Sometimes I mix home cooked egg food with dry commercial egg food for an extra boost. I stir until it is dryish and crumbly. Other times they get it "straight."

I also sprinkle their vitamins and supplements over the fresh food, now that "everyone" eats it. If they did not all eat it, I would put the vitamins in their water instead. This is not my preferred method because additives can cause the water quality to deteriorate rather quickly, and because we can't observe their intake as well with vitamins in the water.

The amount of food that a finch eats in a day is quite small. Since cooked and raw foods tend to spoil after a few hours, serve only a teaspoon or two per bird. Replenish later in the day if needed.

Never leave finches without access to food; their bodies have an extremely high metabolism and they need constant fuel.

A Daily Diet Snapshot

Here's what I normally do in the bird room each day.

Morning: Provide fresh egg or egg food / veggie chop /sprouts on small paper plates. If it's a vitamin day, I sprinkle vitamins over it. Nearly every day I sprinkle probiotics on the food. Probiotics cannot be overdone, and they're always beneficial.

I used to limit the amount of food I gave them, since we know a finch eats about 1/2 teaspoon of food. Now I don't limit the fresh food; they can eat all they want.

On Sundays, I also add calcium to the water.

While they are eating, I walk around and do my morning "well check." I carefully look into each cage, mentally counting the residents. I watch them: Are they acting normal? Is anyone fluffed, or sleeping when they normally wouldn't? In this way I can catch illness or other problems early so that they can be given treatment or go to the vet. Often a bird that's just fluffed, with no visible symptoms, responds to a day or two in the hospital cage with heat and electrolytes.

Afternoon/early evening: Remove the paper plates. Make sure there is dry egg food (if there are young in the cage) and the dry food mix. These are in separate feeders from the seed, I have never tried to mix them. I might provide more fresh food at this point, sometimes home-grown parsley or some other fruit or vegetable. I take down the drinkers and replace with clean ones if I haven't already. After they've eaten most of the fresh food, I'll top off seed feeders. If I do it too early, they will switch to seed instead of eating whole foods so most times this chore is done late in the day.

Encouraging Picky Eaters to Try New Foods

Many finches arrive having come from a background of an all-seed diet, so they do not want to try new foods. They are afraid of them. At our house we describe this as "everything is a monster." Remember - in their hearts they are the prey of everything on the planet. By introducing them to non-threatening foods first, it is possible to entice your feathered friends to try new foods. For each of the methods described below, be sure to offer the food for several days in a row without expecting any results (yes, you will waste some food). Try to offer them at the same time and in the same type of container every day. It only takes about 1/2 teaspoon per finch.

Most birds love dry commercial egg food, so if you have not already tried it, offer that first. After serving this in a treat cup or on a plate on the cage floor for awhile, try adding a fruit or vegetable: Corn, bits of cooked rice, or peas are all small and easily given. Shredded broccoli is a favorite. Once they start eating these, you can slowly introduce more foods. If the dry egg food "accidentally" spreads over the vegetable, it can be tasted and perhaps enjoyed.

Another way to entice birds to eat unfamiliar foods is by using teacher birds that you know will eat them. Finches are flock birds, so if one eats a food the others will follow. Look outside the Gouldian family - a zebra finch, canary, or society finch will usually eat greedily. Even though you may not house them together, if the finches in a nearby cage are within view and eating eagerly, the Gouldians will soon follow suit.

The next method is not my favorite, because of the possibility of starving a finch, but it can be useful. Early in the morning is when Gouldians are hungriest, remove seed hoppers and other foods, and serve only the fresh food or pellets you are trying to introduce. After an hour or so, no more than two hours, return the foods they are used to back to the aviary *whether or not they have eaten the newer food*. This method could easily backfire if a busy person forgot to return the feeders, so proceed with the utmost caution. Keep doing this every morning until you see results.

Birds become accustomed to what you give them, so if they are not used to eating fresh foods, serve the same ones each day over a period of time. A chop is ideal for this (see the recipes section) because once they are comfortable with chop, you can vary the ingredients without the finches rejecting the entire chop.

Here's how people with parrots convert from a seed-only to a fresh diet. I will outline the plan with my own adaptation for smaller species:

Each day place four dishes in the cage. One contains healthy pellets, one a seed mix, one water and the fourth fresh food mixed with 50% seed or dry egg food. The bird will not eat the fresh food; that's okay. You are getting him used to being served.

As soon as you notice the bird eating the seed *out of the fresh food bowl*, remove the seed dish. Now there are three dishes in the cage. Keep the one you removed out of the cage during the day but put it back in late in the afternoon. This will be your routine for at least two weeks, up to a month. Be sure to continue to provide pellets, and keep the 50/50 ratio mentioned above in the fresh mix.

Once he eats consistently from the seed/fresh food mix, slowly decrease the amount of seed in the mix.

Continue this each month until you have reached the ratios of food you prefer.

After that, offer seeds separately from the vegetables but in small amounts; finches will eat what they like best, and seeds are what they like. Some people only provide seed every other day. I give seeds daily but at the end of the day, after they've already eaten fresh foods and egg food.

Finally, the Recipes

Here's a detailed way of making chop, in case you haven't done one before, you're very busy and time is limited, or you're just a person who likes to follow a recipe.

Easy First Chop

About 8 eggs, hard boiled and shells removed (reserve shells for later use)

1 large bag frozen mixed veggies (carrots, green beans, peas, corn and/or cauliflower)

1-2 cups fresh kale or spinach

½ apple, chopped or apple juice or apple sauce. If you never have these on hand, buy a 6-pack of children's apple sauce cups and add one container. It's a perfect size, and you can recycle the container as a feeder. They last a long time without refrigeration.

1 c Roudybush pellets soaked in the apple juice or in water

½ c dry commercial egg food mixture

Put pellets in a 2-cup measure and add liquid to soak. Put eggs on to boil. While eggs boil, thaw the vegetables in the microwave and chop the veggies and apple. I throw these in the food processor to chop, then dump into a big bowl. Next I put the soaked pellets and egg food in the food processor and chop those, keeping them in the bowl. Then I remove the shells from the eggs, throw the eggs in the chopper...don't chop too much or they are like paste. Just whirl to mix with the pellets. Put in bowl and stir to mix. Save the eggshells to grind later, or grind and add to this food. (My flock prefer them separate) Press the mixture into ice cube trays. You can get ice trays at the dollar store. I found some inexpensive silicone trays with teeny sections that are perfect, and it's easier to pop the cubes out. They're linked at www.GouldianGardens. com/book_links.

I used to put one container in the refrigerator for current use, freeze the rest in ice cube trays, then transfer them to containers or freezer bags. These were perfect for smaller cages. Now I'm feeding a larger amount of fresh food and I discovered something easier. Line a baking sheet with wax paper. Spoon enough chop onto the wax paper to make a thin layer. Spread with the back of a spoon or a spatula until fairly flat, then lay another piece of wax paper on top. Keep layering until all the chop is spread thin, then freeze. When they are frozen, store in bags or plastic containers. These layers are easy to break and also thaw quickly. Thaw before serving, or break off a chunk the night before and thaw overnight in the refrigerator.

"What's in the Fridge" Flexible Chop

(flexible, because you choose what goes in based on what you have on hand)
Cooked couscous, wheat cereal or plain oatmeal
Some of the following, crushed or ground:

THE GOULDIAN FINCH HANDBOOK   103

sesame seeds, sunflower seeds, almonds, twelve grains, flax seeds, chia seeds

Finely chopped kale, dandelion, parsley, carrots, broccoli leaves and/or tops, celery leaves, radish leaves, chard, mustard greens.

Sprouted millet or other types of sprouts. Sprout mixes are fine.

Optional: tiny bit of seedless fruit, such as blueberries, apples, or kiwi.

Directions: In a large bowl, mix all ingredients. If creating a larger batch, a bucket or storage container is useful for stirring. Store in sealed containers or freeze.

I find that Chops are taken better when they are on the dry side. Because of this, I often mix dry eggfood with the mixture just before serving. Breadcrumbs or even plain oatmeal would also work.

Once your birds are used to them, you might be able to serve chops wetter or as whole, unmixed foods. I don't know for sure because I always chop. Zebra finches tend to like to wrestle with the bigger size leaves and chunks; Gouldians want it small. Even my parrots have taken to eating very tiny chop.

Super Duper 7-day Chop

For this you'll need seven food storage containers. Fill each one with any or all of the following.

1 Dark leafy Greens. Try collard greens, parsley, kale, dandelion greens, spinach, wheatgrass.
2 Green vegetables, such as Brussels sprouts, summer squash, green beans, or peas.

3 Shredded carrots, yellow/orange/red peppers including hot, yellow squash, and/or other orange veggies.
4 Soaked oatmeal, millet, quinoa, or pellet food
5 Fresh sprouts. Purchase sprout mixes online or use seeds like broccoli, radish, and wheat. For those who like beans, only Adzuki, Mung, and Garbanzo beans are recommended for finches.
6 Dried mealworms or other insects
7 Frozen mixed veggies, thawed/chopped --fill the rest of the container

Stir well. I freeze half my containers and leave the others in the fridge. To serve, add other fruits vegetables, or seeds, or just add a scoop of seed mix and a scoop of pellets on the side, and you've got the entire meal for the day.

*I realize this sounds like a lot. For a few finches, your "scoop" might be a teaspoon. I use a tablespoon for most small cages, a teaspoon for a pair.

Mom's Busy Day Bird Food Recipe

1 jar baby spinach
1 small bag frozen vegetables, thawed
1 cup cooked couscous, rice, or oatmeal

Stir the vegetables into the rice mixture. Whirl in blender until chopped fine enough for finches.

Sprout Patties

Sprouts (alfalfa, beans, millet, commercial sprouting mix, etc.)
Peas or other greens

Fresh vegetables
Small bit of fruit

Whirl in the blender until mixed. Press out into small patties. Dehydrate at 95 degrees until dry. Use in place of pellet food. (You can dehydrate in a regular oven - if the temperature doesn't show low enough, use an oven thermometer. Long ago I just set mine at the lowest temperature, 200 degrees, and kept the door open a bit.)

Birdie Bread

Bread is a great way to provide nutrition. If you don't want to make your own, search for Bird Bread Mix to purchase online. Birds will usually pick at them; I crumble mine for the finches and leave them in bigger pieces for the bigger birds. Some people use a food processor to grind them into crumbs. You can mix your vitamins right into the crumbled bread, and add boiled egg or commercial egg food for a hearty meal.

Easy Rainy Day Bread

1/2 cup pellet food
1/4 cup wheat germ
1/4 cup cornmeal
4 eggs, with shells or save shells and serve separately
1-1 1/2 cups broccoli, chopped
1 cup shredded carrot and/or mixed vegetables

Mix all ingredients. Pour into a greased baking dish and bake at 350 until done. Cool, then grind in a food processor, or simply cut into portions and serve. Many other chopped veggies can also be added. If adding more dry ingredients, an extra egg or 1/2 cup of applesauce will be needed. This is a great recipe for someone with only a few finches.

Today's Bird Bread

I change my recipe almost all the time, depending on what's on hand. Here's what I am doing this morning.

10 eggs
1 large bag frozen mixed veggies (carrots, green beans, peas)
1.5 cups fresh kale
½ apple, chopped (could also use apple juice or apple sauce)
1 c Roudybush pellets soaked in in water
½ c dry egg food mixture
1 c cornmeal

Crack the eggs into a large bowl and whisk a little. Thaw the vegetables in the microwave and chop the veggies and apple. I throw these in the food processor to chop, then dump into the big bowl and stir. I put the soaked pellets, egg food, and cornmeal in the food processor and chop those, add to big bowl. Stir to mix.

Put all that in a 13X9 pan and cook at 350 until done. Mine usually takes 30 minutes. You want it just brown on top.

I chop the egg shells in a Nutri bullet because it makes a finer grind (no sharp edges) and serve it separately on a dish.

You can cut the bread up into squares and freeze it, pulling out enough to thaw for that day's meal. I serve about a 1-inch square for every 2 birds. Sprinkle vitamins on it if you need to serve them that day. Remember there are vitamins in the pellets and egg food, too.

Healthy 2-step Birdie Bread

Part 1: Dry Mix
Stir together in large bowl:

 1/2 c ground flax seed
 1/2 c ground nuts, whatever is on hand -- pecans, walnuts, or almonds
 1 c almond flour or coconut flour
 1/2 c wheat germ
 1 c corn meal
 1 c pea protein (because we have it on hand; you could use soy)
 2 c oatmeal
 1 c unprocessed bran (can substitute bran cereal)
 1 c soy lecithin
 1/2 c coconut oil

Part 2: Wet Mix
Mix in blender or food processor to a thick puree.

 6 eggs with shell
 2 c shredded carrots
 One apple, peeled and chopped or one banana
 2 c spinach leaves
 1 bell pepper, can also add 1/2 c jalapeno pepper
 1/2 c zucchini
 1 c squash - spaghetti , acorn, butternut etc.
 2 cloves garlic
 1/4 c basil or 1 tsp. dry basil or Italian seasoning

Stir each mix. Add the wet mix to the dry mix. It should have a doughy consistency; add more flour if needed. Press onto an oiled cookie sheet (coconut oil) and bake at 350 for about 1/2 hour. Let cool before slicing into squares; freeze.

Pumpkin Cornbread, Healthy

Mix in one bowl:

> 3 cups corn meal
> 1 cup coconut or almond flour, could also use chickpea flour
> 1/2 cup ground flax
> 3 tablespoons baking powder

Mix in another bowl:

> 2 cups unsweetened coconut milk (in carton, not canned)
> 1/2 cup coconut oil, flaxseed oil, or vegetable oil
> 3-6 eggs, beaten
> 2 cups fresh or canned pure pumpkin puree
> 1 bag frozen mixed veggies thawed and rinsed, chopped fine
> 1 cup chopped greens--kale, chard, collard
> Optional: Up to 3 teaspoons cinnamon, 3 teaspoons ginger, 1/2 teaspoon ground cloves.

Combine the 2 mixes. Pour into (2) greased 13"x 9" pans. Bake 30-45 min at 400 degrees, until a knife comes out clean. If adding green powder supplement, vitamins, calcium, and/or iodine supplements, wait until after baking for best results.

Cut into squares and freeze in baggies.

Mashed Pellets

1/2 banana, mashed
1 small cooked sweet potato
1 egg with shell
1 tbsp. of almond butter
2 tsp unsweetened apple sauce
Pinch of cinnamon

Blend all the above. Combine with 1 cup powdered pellets (powder by running in blender or food chopper) in a bowl and mix until it forms a dough.

Pour into tiny bite-size muffin tins or liners and bake for about 15 mins at 350 degrees. Serve on a small paper plate in the bottom of the cage, whole or crumbled.

Breakfast Pudding for the Little Guys

1 c apple juice
1-2 c water
1/4 c oat groats
1/2 c quinoa
1/2 c millet
1/4 c raisins
1/4 c organic no-salt almonds, sunflower seeds, pecans, or walnuts very finely chopped (whirl in coffee grinder).

Put all ingredients in a pot and bring to a boil. Cover; reduce heat and simmer until creamy, about 30 min. Stir. It's really breakfast pudding; may need to add seeds and dry eggfood to convince them to eat it at first. *Groats are the healthier form of a grain. Substitute any groat for the oat groats if you prefer

Egg Food

"Egg food" is the term used for giving finches serious protein. It's especially important to provide if you are breeding them. It's based around fresh eggs, and often includes eggshells for extra calcium.

World's Easiest Egg Food

4 hard-boiled eggs, peeled
1 container dry bread crumbs, plain

Run the ingredients through the food processor to mix well. Refrigerate. Serve every morning. If you need to be convinced that it is important to feed supplemental foods, this will convince you. Amazingly, it also has a great carbohydrate/protein ratio for birds. And apparently, it's yummy.

Egg Food #2

This is the egg food I make every two weeks.

8-10 eggs (beaten, no shell),
1 cup of soaked Roudybush pellets
1 cup of Roudybush Soak-and-Feed Saraha Sunrise (If you don't have this, just leave it out)
1 cup of dried eggfood, I use Higgins (more at the end, if the mix is too wet)
1/2 cup parsley, fresh or dried
1 cup of kale & carrots shredded, or whatever is on hand
1 bag frozen mixed vegetables - fresh is always best but nothing wrong with these
1-2 cups cooked couscous

To serve as a bread: Mix well and pour into a greased pan. Bake at 400 degrees until set and a wooden toothpick is inserted and comes out clean.

To serve fresh: Leave out the dry eggfood. Boil eggs and mix well into the rest of the ingredients, spoon into ice cube trays, freeze. Upon thawing, mix in the dry egg food and vitamins (if desired). I often serve it without the dry eggfood.

Miscellaneous Recipes

Roasted Pumpkin

Cut the top off one small pumpkin. Scrape out the seeds. Brush inside and outside with coconut oil. Sprinkle on herbs of choice. Bake in the oven at 400 degrees for 30 minutes. Serve.

To add even more nutrition, while baking cut up:

1 green pepper
3-4 carrots
1 cooked sweet potato
Mix with pumpkin and bake 20 more minutes. Cool and serve.

Beans-N-Greens for Birds

1/2 lb beans (Adzuki, Mung, or Garbanzo)
1/2 lb chick starter, commercial egg food, or a can of dry bread crumbs
1 sweet potato
1 head broccoli
Peas
Carrots

Corn
1 apple
1 c green beans
1/2 c brown rice, cooked
1 c pellets
1/2 c whole oats or quinoa

Sprout the beans. While waiting on beans, chop all vegetables small enough for finches. Chop the beans, add to mix. Chop the pellets and fold in along with the dry oats or quinoa. The moisture in the mix will soak the oats or quinoa. Freeze into quart size or smaller bags, or place in ice cube trays and freeze.

5   1+1 Soon Equals a Flock - Breeding

10 Tips for Better Breeding

1. Don't provide a nest until you've owned the birds at least 3 months
2. Have extra cages ready for baby birds
3. Use plastic nest boxes made specifically for finches
4. Provide as much nesting material as they want, which can be a lot
5. It is a myth that birds abandon babies you touch, but...
6. Leave the nest alone as much as possible to prevent abandonment
7. Provide dry egg food at all times for the mother to feed to the babies
8. Check the babies on the 2nd day to see that the parents are feeding them.
9. If a pair continually tosses babies, remove them from the breeding program.
10. Leave babies with parents a minimum of 45 days

The Gouldian Dance

As breeding season nears, an observant enthusiast will notice the males singing more often. Their beaks have a pearly sheen and the rosy tip seems brighter than usual.

Figure 5-1 Male Courtship Dance
© Tina Billings 2020.

They will sing not only to the females, but to other males, young birds, and even their owners. The upright, stiff-necked posture of the male Gouldian finch while singing is a part of his courtship display. During this display, he fluffs his feathers as if to make himself look larger. He stands erect, bowing his head regally while singing. If a hen is present, he may also beak wipe across the perch, shake his beak and head, puff out in front of her, and hop up and down. If the hen is interested, she will shake her tail side to side, and may even twist her tail toward him. If not, she will fly off.

The signs are present: It's breeding season.

When selecting breeding pairs instead of allowing for self-selection, note that hens can store sperm as long as 16 days. It is possible for her to produce multiple fertile eggs after mating; therefore, she should be isolated from other males at least 16 days before setting her up with the chosen cock.

When you Don't Want Babies

A frequently asked question: Whoa! I got some finches and put a nest in their cage, and now they have eggs! I didn't plan to raise babies. What do I do?

Answer: If you don't want babies, do not provide a nest. It is a misconception that birds need a nest for sleeping. They don't. But now you have eggs, so let's address that. The eggs are not necessarily fertile, and they do not become viable until the hen sits on them for several days. So you can throw them out if she is not sitting yet.

The problem with tossing them is that she may keep laying more eggs to replace the ones you are removing. Another issue is that some people feel it's morally wrong to toss out eggs, even those that aren't truly growing yet.

If you feel it's not ethical to throw them away, wait until day 5 and candle the eggs with a strong flashlight. If there is life you will see veins and possibly the heartbeat. If you see nothing except a yellow blob, it is not fertile and you can safely dispose of it.

To Keep Real Eggs but Prevent Them from Hatching

Say your finch keeps laying eggs, but you don't want to have babies. One way to resolve this is to take the eggs and shake them to addle them. Another idea is to refrigerate them or boil them, then return them to the nest. The cold or heat prevents the egg from hatching, but the hen still has her nest full of eggs so she will not continue laying more. Instead she will sit on the eggs for up to 3 weeks, then she'll lose interest and move on.

One method to prevent babies is to replace each egg that she lays with a plastic egg. This also keeps her from laying egg after egg to replace the ones you're tossing. Usually she will only lay one egg per day early in the morning, so each day trade the real egg for a plastic one. She may fill her nest with 5-6 eggs and sit on them for some weeks. Eventually she will stop sitting. By trading out the eggs you've prevented damaging her health with constant egg-laying, but she has satisfied her desire to lay eggs.

People are always surprised to learn that hens lay eggs even when a male is not present. Egg laying is brought on by certain external factors, not the presence of a male. Eggs can be infertile even when a male is present. Likewise, you may witness a pair breeding but never see any eggs produced.

When a hen lays but a male isn't present, she is not having babies but she is still stressing her body by producing eggs. Some ideas for making her stop laying eggs are:

- Lower the light cycle. If your lights are on 14 hours a day, shorten to 13 or less. Keep shortening the cycle every week or so until she stops laying.
- If you can't change the lights, cover the cage for 12 hours at night.
- Rearrange the cage. Move the plants, perches, feeders, and nest boxes.
- Back off on fresh foods.

When to Breed

Breeding Gouldian Finches is a hobby that has many facets. It is always interesting and is fraught with surprises. But at the same time, it is not something to be undertaken frivolously. The care of Gouldians should be studied and understood before beginning to attempt to breed. This chapter should be read and re-read. In fact, many aviculturists believe one should find a mentor and study with them before attempting to breed birds. In this way one can understand Gouldian breeding habits and carefully offer them the proper tools to breed successfully.

Too many people purchase a pair of finches, throw them together in a cage, and allow them to breed without understanding the possible problems they might encounter. Unprepared for tossed chicks or parents that don't feed, the babies and sometimes the parents lose lives unnecessarily. Kudos to the reader for digging into this chapter!

It is best not to breed finches until you've owned them a long time - perhaps up to one year. I say this for many reasons. One, many birds come from pet shops or bird marts where babies are taken just after weaning. Two, they may be able to produce at this age, but it is terribly unhealthy. Breeding a hen under age one year gives her a high risk of becoming egg-bound and also of dying a premature death. Immature males are not helpful to the hen, plus they could toss babies from the nest.

Another consideration is the quarantine protocol. Were the birds systematically taken through it upon their arrival? If not, best to work on getting rid of any parasites or other problems before beginning to breed them.

Let's look more specifically at each element of good breeding practices.

Gouldian Seasons

In the wild, Gouldian finches breed only during the wet season. They do not breed at any other time of year. The internal changes in their bodies take place as a response to signals from their environment. In some species, notably canaries, that would mean extended daylight hours as spring turns into summer, and that is part of it. But with tropical species, the trigger is the sudden availability of grasses and seeds due to the rain. This causes a high level of protein availability, which helps the males produce sperm and the ovaries secrete hormones and develop eggs.

In captivity, finches can theoretically breed all year around, but most people keep each pair down to a maximum of 2 or 3 clutches in order to maintain the health of their stock. Allowing more will compromise the health of the parent birds, particularly the hens. They may experience egg binding, which can be fatal, as well as other health issues. They may not live a full lifespan because of the toll on their bodies.

Breed during the right season if you can figure out when that is. Many breeders in the U.S. feel the birds would normally breed during Australian spring, so they set up their birds for breeding during November to March, which is summer in Australia but winter in the U.S. Because that's backward for us, some breeders choose to set up their pairs in March-June. I have tried both; I assure you that when your birds are ready, they will know it--no matter what time of year it happens to be. Most likely they will breed at the time that is most inconvenient to your schedule.

Pre-Breeding Preparation

Parasite Free

Breeder birds need to be free from parasites, protozoa, and illness. Using the quarantine protocol when first purchasing them assures most of this, unless other birds have come in and out of the aviary or the birds are housed outdoors. In

Whether outdoors or inside, it's always a good idea to treat for mites, worms, and parasites before the breeding season. This ensures the birds are as healthy as they can be while they're raising babies.

Molt

Besides the birds being in excellent condition, the molting process should have ended at least one month earlier. Normally this is not a problem, as molt occurs after the breeding season ends. But occasionally a bird will have a second molt or a slow molt, which could possibly interfere with the breeding season. In this case hold that individual back a bit to let him build up energy.

I believe that there is a set time a Gouldian always molts related to the time of year the finch hatched -- spring or fall. I definitely have spring and fall molters. This used to worry me –I thought one of them could miss out on getting a mate because he was molting. But with the use of the Austerity Cycle, their bodies can be tricked into breeding condition, and molt will follow the breeding season.

Note: We aren't talking about the first molt here - birds under one year old are not mature enough to care for young, and young hens may be more likely to become egg bound than their older counterparts. The molt I'm referring to is the annual shedding and replacing of feathers.

To complicate matters, the Gouldian is one species that can speed up or slow down their molt. In the wild, we see this as a response to lack of a seed supply. There can be reasons for it in captive birds as well, such as illness, over breeding, poor diet, and/or weather conditions. And sometimes they'll even have a second molt. So molt does play a role in the breeding cycle and is worth considering when setting up birds to breed. They won't care for babies if they are molting.

Age and Other Factors

Breeding pairs must be unrelated. If getting them from a breeder, he or she should have some method of recording families. With a large flock, this is accomplished by banding the birds by family, which we'll discuss at length later in this chapter. All breeders (the birds, not the people) should also be free of any physical defects that could be genetic, no matter how tempting it is to breed them. This includes baldness. And of course, they must be extremely healthy -- building nests, laying eggs, and raising chicks is hard work.

The age of the bird is important. I see many new owners attempting to breed Gouldians that either are just past their first molt, or are of unknown age because they came from a pet shop. Pet shops often receive young babies to sell, so it's likely their birds are six to twelve months old. Sure it's tempting to go ahead and try to breed them, but younger birds are more likely to become egg bound, toss babies, and be poor parents. Better to wait until the next year when the results are more likely to be positive. They "can" breed before they are a year old, but they're better as breeders if you wait until age 14 months. Some reputable breeders wait as late as two years before attempting to breed the pairs.

Breeding is hard on finches' bodies. Prior to breeding, the males and females should be separated for time. This will give them a chance to rest and restore energy before the next breeding season begins. They are best rested when they cannot see one another. If cages are in the same room, a simple cardboard barrier will suffice.

To build their strength, begin feeding vitamins, supplements, and fresh foods if you haven't been. By using the protein-rich diet outlined in Chapter 4, the birds can be brought into condition. This is often referred to as the abundance diet or flush diet. It consists of soft food, soaked seed, and extra millets or other grass seeds. Hens will need extra calcium and phosphorus. Calcium and phosphorus should always be given in the correct ratio, 1:2. Using boiled egg, chopped with the shell and blended with the soft food, as part of their regimen will go a long way in providing the calcium needed.

Austerity and Separation

Over the past 20 years or so, many people have turned to mimicking nature by way of diet. They feel this creates the most 'natural' life cycle. In Australia, the native home of Gouldian finches, diet is controlled by the seasons, rain, and temperature. There is an austerity period where little food is available, followed by a rise in temperature and a wet season that produces seeds and insects. The abundance of foodstuffs during the wet season brings on the breeding season in Gouldians.

To mimic the austerity season, reduce feeding to a basic seed mix, with no or very little green food. This should coincide with the time at which you would separate the males from females for a resting period.

Once it is "breeding season," usually four to eight weeks later, pair the birds and slowly increase the green foods, egg food or insects, and other nutrients.

The advantage of an austerity season is that it helps to reduce the hormones. One breeder said practicing this seasonal change was the best decision he had made for his aviary. When the austerity season is over, the birds will all molt and begin breeding at the same time - a synchronized aviary instead of having babies here and there, nearly non-stop from January through November. This will also reset those hens that insist on laying eggs for months on end.

The Effect of Light Hours and Temperature

Breeding is easiest in most parts of the United States during the late spring and summer months. This gives birds the benefit of having many hours of daylight, and less temperature variation in most areas. Conversely, breeding during shorter daylight hours may produce smaller, less healthy chicks. For birds kept indoors, good full-spectrum lighting set on timers can replace long sunlight hours.

It is possible bring them into breeding mode artificially. To produce a breeding cycle, increase the light to 14 hours of "daylight" and change to a high-protein diet with a lot of fresh foods. It is actually the abundant protein (food availability) that pushes them into breeding condition. Many people do this with success.

The "experts," whoever they are, say that you must set up for breeding when temperatures are 73 to 77 degrees F (23-25 C). It is usually much warmer than that in my climate, so I believe that Gouldians are adaptable and will come into breeding season with appropriate light, humidity, and good nutrition. The preferred minimum temperature for the breeding room is 65 degrees Fahrenheit, and warmer is always better.

Setting up the Cage or Aviary

A breeding cage or aviary doesn't differ much from the day-to-day setup. You'll need nest boxes and greenery (either live or fake). A breeding cage will have feed cups and drinkers, an extra cup or two for fresh food and the calcium supplement of choice--cuttlebone, F-vite, mineral grit, and/or eggshell. A hen who is laying eggs turns over her blood calcium four times per hour -- she must have plenty of protein and calcium available at all times in order to lay successfully.

Place a nest or nest box in the cage as high as possible. Give some thought to the way the nest box will be hung; hanging one outside the cage allows for egg checks without so much disturbance, and it takes up less indoor space. But this makes it more accessible to children and predators, plus some cages do not have the door necessary for a nest box.

Most owners prefer a plastic nest box because of the ease of cleaning. These usually have a hinged lid that can be lifted for egg checks. If breeding multiple pairs in a colony, place more nests in the aviary than you have birds.

The Set-up: Colony or Pair?

Should you colony breed, or separate the pairs out for breeding? The answer is: it depends.

In order to successfully breed a colony, the aviary must not be overcrowded to start. You will find that, once the birds have begun mating, they seem to bicker--a lot. So if it is already crowded there may be problems like plucking, chasing, and so on. It won't quite be the serene environment you envisioned when setting up the aviary!

The minimum flight for colony-type breeding is 4X3X6 feet or longer. The bigger the better.

If competition is noticed from other species of birds--owl finches, society finches, canaries and so on--it would be best to remove them from the flight altogether. The competition may concern nest boxes or nesting materials. In fact, one study showed that breeding in a self-colony composed of all Gouldian finches yielded three times more young than when the Gouldians shared the colony with other species.[3]

Some breeders provide two nest boxes per pair of birds. Place all the nests at the same height if at all possible. Space them out as far as you can while still creating a place for them to perch, room to fly, etc. I don't provide two per pair, since my "colonies" are just double cages, but I put in one or two more nest boxes than pairs, depending on how many pairs are in the flight. If some seem less than content, I might add another box. My yellow-headed male, Banjo, at this moment seems to have three nest boxes all to himself - meaning I have to add extra boxes to make up for his greed.

I like to place silk or plastic plants in the cage around the nest boxes so that the birds feel hidden from the others. This will, hopefully, prevent them from trying to defend the nest by chasing the other birds away. I did an experiment by placing fake plants around some nest boxes and not others. The ones that were closely surrounded by plants at the opening were selected first. Some that were open to another nest on the adjacent wall or directly across were completely ignored. Adding more plants as a visual barrier solved the problem.

In a colony, supply at least two perches, two drinkers, and two feeding areas. To help things move along quicker, place some nesting material in each nest. Put the rest of the available nest material in a small box on the floor where the birds can get to it, or in a small-animal plastic hay rack. Be careful that it is not located directly under a perch or it will become soiled.

If the breeder birds have not yet been introduced, place between three and five pairs into the aviary *at the same time.* They will pair off.

If some of the Gouldians do not seem interested, remove them from smaller enclosures after a week or so. They'll become the target of zealous pairs otherwise.

Breeding One Pair to a Cage

Colony breeding can be done, but if your aviary is small it can be stressful for the pair trying to breed. Some will chase others at various periods during the process, sometimes claiming an entire half of the flight cage for their own. Also, in cases of chicks that differ in age, a fledgling could enter the nest of hatchlings out of curiosity, and either be injured by the parents or injure the babies in the nest. Because of this, it might be better to remove the breeding pair to smaller separate cage. Besides, in cages you can control who mates with whom. It is worth noting that in the wild nests are often found miles away from any other Gouldian nest so for those who wish to emulate wild breeding, you might choose individual cage breeding.

A cage's size is not terribly important in this instance because they will not be in it forever. It should be freshly disinfected, and the floor may be covered with sand, or another suitable material like newspaper or hay, perhaps mixed with grit and shaved cuttlebone. They seem to especially love foraging for the cuttlebone on the floor. If you are accustomed to using cages with grates on the floor, these are acceptable; however, consider the young that could be tossed from the nest. Limbs or necks can be broken upon falling through the grate. Using flat flooring covered in substrate like wood shavings or sand without the grate could save a life. Even placing newspaper over the grate will work.

Do not provide too many perches in a small cage. They only need two, positioned so that they must fly longways from one to the other for exercise. If the nest box does not have a perch mounted on it, I usually put the highest perch right beside the nest box. I find the parent birds enjoy being able to stand on it and peek in.

Put the nest box and breeding materials in place before you introduce a bird to the new quarters. Put the hen or the cock in next. Whichever one you choose, let that one settle in for a few days before introducing the prospective mate. Placing them side by side or at least where they can see each other allows them to get to know one another before they have to live in the same cage. Read on for some thoughts about which bird should go in first.

Which Bird Do I Put In The Breeding Cage First?

When this question was put to breeders, the answers were just about evenly divided. They might put the hen in because

   .... She will check out the nest site
   .... Her emotional health is more important
   .... That's the way their mentor did it.

Others might put the cock in first because.

.... He will search out a nest site
.... It is more important that he become comfortable so they will breed
.... He is the one building the nest.

Both sides felt strongly about their reasons for choosing either the cock or the hen to go first -- which means it probably doesn't matter. I have been cage breeding this year, and I put the hens into the cages just moments before putting the males in. I cannot say there were any problems at all in doing it this way. However, in the wild the cock bird would go out and find the nesting spot -- so you might want to start with the male. Do what works for you.

Birds' Readiness

"Hens are ready to breed when their beaks have turned black" --this is a commonly made statement, but some hens (notably yellow and silver mutations) do not get a black beak. With those, watch their behavior instead. If she is interested in the dancing male, she may puff out her own chest and dance. She might sit and watch his behavior, or beak-wipe-- this indicates she is accepting him as a mate. She could even lean forward in breeding position and quiver her tail. If she continually flies off -- they're not a match.

Sometimes pairs do not, well, pair up. One bird may not respond to the other, or one is too aggressive. They may beak-fence. Often a hen isn't quite ready yet and they need to be separated for a week or two.

If this behavior extends beyond an initial day or two, it is safest to assume the pair is not a match and remove the male. Leaving a pair like this together only results in injury and frustration; you cannot force them to get along.

On the other hand, it is possible to give up too quickly -- allowing the birds time to get to know one another works best except in the case of aggression.

Many types of finches and other species mate for life; however, most Gouldian finches pair only for the mating season. They may produce two or three broods in that season, then split and find other partners for the next. This is useful for the breeder, who can re-pair them in order to produce many color mutations. That said, I have several pairs that have remained together for years.

When breeding selectively, most breeders have an idea of which birds they want to put together. If you normally keep males and females together, be aware that some may select a mate before you pair them up. No amount of coaxing will get these birds to switch to other partners, even if you move them to separate breeding cages! In this case, it is best to let them have their way, or put them back in the aviary to wait until next season.

I allow my birds to select their own partners, since this usually leads to a more solid pairing - and more babies. I have just put sixteen birds back into the colony cage after a rest. I have 4 pairs so far, of which three are the same pairing as last year and one is new. The hen in question was a fairly new bird at the end of last season and did not have a mate. The male's previous mate is now un-mated. Interestingly, this newer hen looks more like him than the previous one; studies show that hens usually choose males that are colored like themselves. Yes, you read that right – the hens choose their own partners.[xvii]

Nests and Nesting

The actual nest, in the wild, is not well-built. It is usually made from grasses. It may be thin and may even be constructed in a low bush. We want to simulate this as closely as possible for our caged birds, not the poorly built nest, of course, but the construction style, by offering them grasses and grass-like material. At the same time, we can improve upon their habits by placing the nest up high, and by perhaps starting the nest process ourselves with a handful of clean grass, hay, or coconut fiber.

Selecting a Nest for Home Use

So you've decided to take the plunge; you're going to breed finches. The first thing you'll need is a nest (well, after a male and female Gouldian). Time to run to the local pet store and get a few nests, right?

Sorry, no. Gouldians do not do well with the small woven nests that you find at the local pet store. Besides the cute, readily available woven nests made from rattan are made to hang inside the cage. They are difficult to look inside of for nest checks, and it is nearly impossible to extract a single egg or hatchling. They are not the favorite of Gouldians, and they soil easily with no sure way to clean them up.

The woven nests are acceptable if there is nothing else available, and if you will consider them a temporary accessory that can be tossed out after use. I say that because they can harbor bacteria, even after a good washing. It doesn't take many of these $3-$6 purchases to realize you're better off paying $12 or $15 for the bigger, more permanent plastic nesting boxes.

Woven nests have another problem. The opening is narrow so the birds have trouble getting in and out. Plus there have been a few reports that the edge can scrape a finch's leg.

I found it useful, back in the beginning, to purchase a medium or large-size wicker nest and fasten it at an angle. This way the babies can have a little more space in the bottom. It works especially well if the opening is tilted so the chicks cannot fall out.

Everyone has their preferences as to which nest box is "best." Generally a deeper one (as opposed to longer) is recommended. The thinking is that the parents are less likely to toss the chicks if it's harder for them to lift them out. I personally find that if they want to remove a chick from the nest, they're going to find a way. And really, do you want a chick that is "contaminated" ruining the health of its siblings? I didn't think so. That's often why they toss chicks, because they are ill or dead and they want to save the family.

Many breeders recommend a box 5X4X5 inches. This is plenty big and has extra depth to keep the babies inside. It is roomy even for larger clutches, and if there's a perch on the front the parents will love you; it allows them to peek in on the babies without disturbing them.

My personal choice is a nest box made of wood or plastic. It can have either a small hole for entry or a half-open front panel. Some even have a front porch. Gouldians in particular do seem to enjoy a perch on the front of their box; they use it to stand watch over the nest.

Some of these nest boxes are made to hang on the outside of the cage so that you are not taking up valuable flying space with them. They usually open at the top, so that you can check the eggs without disturbing anyone. And outside nest boxes are great for videography and photography—but they're also more accessible to children and predators. So consider where the nest box would be out of harm's way.

Boxes made of plastic are the most useful in my opinion, because they can be washed, sanitized, and reused. Wooden boxes are nice, but difficult to sanitize. Wood boxes should be cleaned in the same manner as wooden perches and allowed to thoroughly dry—in the sun if possible.

Many people also create their own nest boxes from cardboard, cartons, or leftover oatmeal boxes. These are fine as long as they are only used one time, then tossed out for sanitary reasons.

My favorite nesting box has repositionable hangers to hang either inside the cage or outside. It is made from plastic — even though I love the wooden ones, I can easily clean plastic while nestlings are present. The other reason is that they're very lightweight, so they are easier to secure to the cage. The drawback to these is that you can lose the clips easily, and no one seems to carry spare clips. My solution to this is to use twist ties. Actually, I bought a whole roll of the stuff in the flower arranging department. You can bend it into a "u" shape, slip it around a cage bar, slide one end into the hole on the nest box, then twist it shut. Repeat for the other side, and you have a very secure nest.

Sometimes you want to hang a nest box on the outside of a cage, but there's no access door. you will need to decide whether you would like to saw out some of the cage bars in order to place your nest box. You only need a very small hole — so only about 3 bars need to be disturbed.

I have done all of the following at one time or another: Cut out holes in the sides of smaller cages, then had to cover them with cardboard later; hung both wooden and plastic boxes inside the cage; and hung them outside at an access door. All systems work for me, except being 5'3" tall I can't always reach all the way to the very back of a large cage to a nest, so I prefer to have them on the outside of the cage. That said, right now about half my nests are inside the cages. I rely on a tall spouse to perform nest checks.

If you cut the bars in order to make room for a nest box on the outside of the cage and change your mind later, it is easy enough to put cardboard over the hole. Use a hole punch or sharp scissors and make 2 holes in the cardboard. Lay it over the hole. Secure it top and bottom with zip ties. None of my Gouldians have ever bothered it. If you have free-roaming larger birds or cats, it is possible they might remove the cardboard.

One word of caution is needed here. Fellow breeders say plastic boxes heat up quickly and do not provide much air flow. Mine have ventilation holes in the top and bottom, but I cover the bottom with paper towels and nesting material. If outdoor birds seem too hot or there are several nestling deaths, this would be something to consider. Indoor birds are probably safe with the plastic nests boxes.

Nesting material

It is essential to the nesting process that the pair has access to appropriate nesting materials. To further complicate matters, you will find that what is 'suitable' will vary from one bird to the next!

In the wild, Gouldians build nests from grasses. If you know without a doubt that your grass has not been chemically treated, it is acceptable to give them grass to use for nesting.

I have used all of the following

- Cotton bits
- Coconut fibers
- Raffia

THE GOULDIAN FINCH HANDBOOK   133

- Burlap
- Jute, unraveled into threads
- Sisal
- Newspaper shreds

Please avoid: small synthetic yarn, hay if you don't know the source, dirt, hair, eucalyptus leaves, and corn cob bedding. Recently, dryer lint has been suggested but I don't recommend it myself. I once placed clean, freshly clipped dog hair in three nest boxes, and the next day all three pairs had covered the hair with paper shreds. "Not acceptable," they seemed to say.

There are packages of "nesting material" available at Big Box stores in the U.S. that contain small white threads, and they are very unsafe for finches and canaries. Little legs can easily become entangled in the threads, and a bird could lose a leg, or you could lose a baby if it isn't found. Better to buy the separate materials and create your own bedding.

My personal favorite material to use is bits of burlap, which I cut into 2" squares then pull the threads to make a stack that I place inside the aviary in a large shallow dish. Every time the dish is nearly empty, I add a fresh batch.

I will not use the thin, long sisal threads; we found a baby trapped in his nest because that had tangled around his leg. That was enough for me to say never again.

Coconut fibers seem to be a hit with the Society Finches more so than the Gouldians. Jute rope purchased from Wal-Mart, unwound into separate strands, also will work well. Tissue is not something I will use, as it was not a favorite of any of my birds. Colored paper shreds from a dollar store look festive and are safe for birds.

My favorite mix: newspaper shreds from the shredding machine, burlap strands, jute strands, and timothy hay.

I put a clean paper towel in the bottom of the box and place a handful of nesting material in it to help them get started, although some of my experienced cocks toss it out and start over. Some people feel that Gouldians are not strong nest-builders, so they put lots of material in the nest box and smash it down in the center with a fist. Either way, supply plenty of extra in a box or bowl so they can decorate the nest themselves.

6 Eggs, Anyone?

Most pairs do not start laying right away. They will get to know each other, go through a period of courtship, and if they find one another suitable they'll begin to build the nest. You may find that only the male builds the nest, but often the hen helps.

Eventually the pair will mate, either inside the box where you will not see it, on the perch, or the cage floor. You will begin to observe them carrying nesting material into the nest. In the wild they would use harder grasses for the first layer of the nest and softer grasses in the center. We try to mimic that in the choices that we offer them; line the nest yourself with handfuls of zoysia, then offer them fine fescue and Kentucky Bluegrass to finish it up. (see the section on nesting for more ideas for nesting materials).

Eggs won't necessarily follow despite your best efforts, but you can expect eggs as early as 15 days after introducing the pair. Some can take considerably longer, especially if one member of the pair was not quite in breeding condition yet. And a few will never produce eggs at all despite the nearly continual nest building.

But assuming we're successful, the hen will lay one white egg early each morning. Do not expect either bird to sit on the eggs until they have all been laid. They simply won't. It is important to remember that the birds know better than we do about their environment. Let them decide whether it's time to sit on the eggs or not, and do not stress about it.

Eggs are viable up to 7 days after laying, so you have that much time for the pair to decide to sit on them, or for you to move the eggs to foster parents. However, because of the time that elapses between eggs, the development of embryos will take longer in some than others; hence, hatching can take as much as two or three days.

Once she's finished laying or there are at least 3 eggs in the nest, both birds will begin sitting "tight." This means one of them is on the nest at all times. They will probably share duties. The female remains in the nest at night and generally the male sits on the eggs during the day. They relieve each other from time to time; you may see one sitting while the other comes out for breakfast, for example. In a colony cage, one may sit inside the nest while the other guards the doorway to discourage eager visitors. Many pairs sit together - and I find those turn out to be the most attentive parents.

How Long Will It Take?

I usually count on at least one week for them to mate, and then five to seven days for egg production. Gouldian hens do not become pregnant, nor do they "carry" egg; rather, they produce them. You will only see one egg per day added to the nest. A total of four to eight eggs is usually laid. So from the time they have been paired, about three weeks will pass, two weeks to sit on eggs, and then from hatch to fledging is about another three weeks.

I have had a nest of thirteen eggs; of those, 9 hatched and seven made it to adulthood. With more than six, it's possible that they all won't get incubated properly. How are all those eggs going to fit under one hen? Some can be fostered out if there's another hen currently sitting. There's more on fostering near the end of this chapter.

Sometimes eggs appear outside the nest. If you are a first-time finch owner, it may be shocking to see eggs on the bottom of the cage. This happens, due to hens not having a nest, or missing the nest (maybe they don't realize what an egg is?). If you touch the egg and the shell is extremely fragile, your hen may be calcium deficient. Supplement her quickly with extra calcium. The blood calcium turns over 4 to 5 times per hour when[4] hens are laying.

Should you put an egg from the floor into the nest? You can if you want. It's impossible to know right away whether it will be a viable egg or not.

Once they begin to sit, be sure to record the dates of laying, incubation, and the expected hatch date (day16). It is amazing how we say we'll remember, and a couple weeks later we don't. Record keeping is important for our own benefit but also can help our buyers if we sell the babies. They will want to know the age, parentage, and so forth.

Are They Fertile?

Clear or infertile eggs sometimes happen. With first season hens, it's like the warm-up for the real thing. Some hens never lay infertile eggs, but others regularly lay 3 or

4 clear eggs before the main event. Some lay clear eggs because they're not all the way in condition yet. Others are in breeding condition, which leads to nesting and then laying, but she wasn't with the male, or she simply didn't breed. Hens without males around can lay eggs as well.

If a hen is *consistently* laying clear eggs, the diet is usually to blame. Supplements in particular should be assessed to be sure the hen is receiving adequate nutrition to support egg-laying as well as caring for chicks. The second most common reason is that she's getting past breeding age.

It's impossible to know immediately whether eggs are fertile or not. We have to wait patiently until the birds have been sitting tight for at least 3 days. For novices, I'd recommend waiting 5 days.

To visually check eggs, wash hands before handling them and be BRIEF. In order to keep from transferring oils from your hands onto the permeable eggshell, you can use a small spoon to lift them from the nest. The egg color will change over time; a fresh egg is white, a fertile egg has a rosy pinkish cast by the 7th day, and an infertile egg turns a yellowish beige color. Fertile eggs have a sheen. Most people will agonize over the fertility with their first birds, but soon learn to recognize the colors and what they mean.

How to Candle an Egg

We candle eggs in order to determine whether they are fertile. To do it, use a bright flashlight or egg candler - dim the lights or carry the egg to a darker room. To candle without touching, it's easiest to look at the eggs with the overhead lights out, holding the candling light in the nest right beside each egg. An egg can also be held in one hand over the light, cupping around it so the egg is backlit.

Place the light source against the side of the egg away from you, always at the end with an air bubble. Wrap one hand around the light source if needed, so that it only shines through the egg and not around it. If the egg has been incubated five days or more, you should be able to see blood vessels and possibly a heartbeat. Infertile eggs contain a yellow yolk sac and an air pocket. Fertile eggs seem to glow pinkish and have red veins.

As the growth progresses the shape of the embryo becomes apparent. Once eggs are candled and determined to be viable, they are best left alone, although it is tempting to keep candling to watch the chick's development!

If eggs are unfertilized (clear upon candling) it doesn't indicate complete lack of success. You can simply try again. It may be that the two birds are young, the pair is incompatible, or they've been disturbed in some way. They may not have bred prior to nesting, or it didn't "take." They may have waited too long before sitting. Sometimes it is an issue you simply can't fix, like exposure to heat, age, infection, tumor, handicap, or obesity.

Should you Remove Infertile Eggs?

Once the nest is full, many people want to take away infertile eggs. There are two schools of thought on egg removal. Leaving them "as mother nature would" is one. This ensures the eggs aren't accidentally shaken, dropped, or contaminated by hands. On the other hand, if an egg is dead in shell or infertile and left touching viable eggs, it could contaminate them.

Some people feel that it's useful to candle eggs and diligently remove them if needed. It helps keep the nest sanitary, they like to know what's going on, and they can hopefully circumvent problems as they arise. The problem with this approach is that it often results in abandoned nests.

So upon finding infertile eggs in the nest, here is the best plan I have found:

- If you're sure the birds have been sitting tight *on all the eggs* for at least 7 days, go ahead and candle, removing infertile eggs. Remember that some eggs were laid later than others and may not appear fertile yet.
- If there are some hatchlings present with a few eggs still unhatched, leave them for several days. The eggs help to raise the chicks off the floor of the nest, preventing them from being squished to death.
- If the hatchlings are one week old and there are still eggs, go ahead and take them out. Most breeders cut them open to see if they were dead in shell, and how far along the development was.

I try to keep my hands out of nests. I usually leave eggs in the nest to provide cushioning for the fertile eggs. And I once made a mistake in candling– I determined there were only three viable eggs in a nest, but four hatched!

For those practicing a completely hands-off system, it's best not to disturb the nest until you believe the eggs have hatched (16 days). You should hear the hatchlings chirping when they're only a few days old.

Nest Checks

Once eggs are laid and birds are sitting tight, don't hover. Give them plenty of privacy to encourage them to practice their best birdie behavior. Finches that get too much attention can abandon the nest.

Sometimes the chick dies in the shell. The change is visible in the outer egg as the shell becomes more of a beige color, with the yolk appearing brownish. Candling the egg reveals a yellow or red yolk without visible signs of life. If the embryo was in the advanced stages, it may seem to sink down against one side of the shell.

Many people want to know why the chick has died in the shell. It can be due to so many things: Parents not sitting properly, temperature and humidity variations, illness, too much handling. A veterinarian can test for signs of illness like staph or e. coli. Eggs that are shaken early on will be addled and not hatch. Late in the cycle, the baby could be positioned in such a way that he can't pip or can't breathe air. Sometimes there is so much calcium that the shell is too hard for a chick to crack.

Despite the enduring myth our mothers told us, it's okay to touch baby Gouldians and eggs in the nest. If you have to clean the nest or move a bird, do so. Just don't touch them unnecessarily.

Manipulating Hatch Time

Some breeders feel that the youngest hatchling gets pushed aside by the bigger, stronger ones; he becomes the loser in the competition for food. To counteract this, breeders artificially change the environment so that all eggs hatch at the same time. I've mentioned this earlier in the chapter, but here's how.

When the first egg is laid, take it away from the hen. Store it in a safe place, like a small box lined with tissue, an empty nest box, or a brooder that is *not turned on*. Keep removing eggs until she has laid 4 or even 5; then

How to Know When Eggs Are Hatching

Around day 16, you may notice the parents flying in and out of the nest, staring at the eggs, or pecking at them. They can hear the chicks peeping. It's hatch time! The chick begins pecking at the perimeter of the shell, a job which can take all day. It is tempting to help the chicks as you see them hatching but don't. His body needs to strengthen by doing all the work of hatching. Though it seems slow and laborious to us, it is an 'honest day's labor' to the bird.

The parents may eat the eggshells, or toss them out of the nest. Don't worry about what they are doing and don't bother them much. *They will not feed the babies* for the first day or so because the babies have a yolk sac which will be absorbed into the body. This is nutrition for the bird just like when it was in the shell. The parents will begin feeding when it is time.

Unhatched eggs should be left alone; remember they were laid on different days, so they may hatch on different days. After four or five days you will have to decide whether to remove them or not. For example, say there are 5 eggs in the nest. Two have hatched. When 5 more days have passed, it is safe to assume the remaining eggs will not hatch.

Be sure to record the hatch date of each chick. I keep a spreadsheet with parents' names, their band information, and each chick. Even if it dies I record it so I can look for trends over time.

Is it necessary to know when the eggs hatch? To me it is. By knowing whether they've hatched and observing the parents' behavior, the breeder will know whether they are feeding their young, and what day to put on the babies' closed leg bands. Notes can also be made about how many chicks hatch and the date they might fledge. It is sort of a maddening time for the breeder, as it is so exciting to have new hatchlings, yet one cannot see them much nor do anything with them for three more weeks!

Hatchlings are naked, having smooth pinkish skin. The roofs of their mouths contain a variety of dark markings (birdie hieroglyphics!) and beside the corners of the beaks you will notice a set of nodules. The nodules are important for the parents because in nature their nests are built in dark, hollow logs. When the parents feed the young, the nodules help guide them to see the mouths.

Figure 6-1 Yellow back baby

The nodules, properly termed papillae, are important to breeders because by observing the color the breeder can determine which color the bird will be. On a green-back baby the outer two nodules are pearlescent blue and the center one is yellowish. For a blue back, the center nodule appears white. For a yellow baby, because the black pigment is blocked the roof of the mouth is not dark; the outer two nodules show pearly white. The center nodule remains the same color as the skin around it. On an ino chick, all nodules appear white.

Figure 6-2 Blue-back baby

You will not hear the babies chirping until at least 4 days and maybe as long as a week. The parents will stay in the nest and feed them up until about Day 10, when they can spend a little more time off the nest because the babies are beginning to grow feathers.

As mentioned, causing the parents to become nervous may lead to abandoned eggs. Nest checks are extremely stressful. Try to limit those to:

- One week after incubation has begun (to be sure nothing is amiss)
- One or two days after the expected hatch date (to count babies and be sure they're getting fed)
- Eight days after hatching to band babies
- If not banding, check on the eighth day anyway to be sure the chicks are healthy and fed, and that there are no dead babies in the nest.

Do I Clean the Nest, or Not?

This is one of the most common questions and the answer is: it depends. If your birds are extremely nervous, are first-time parents, or are suspicious of you being near the nest, leave it. You run a great risk of causing them to abandon the nest by messing with it -- and it's not worth it.

If your birds seem confident and are comfortable with you and your movements around their nest, clean it out quickly and put the babies back right away. Here's how.

Cleaning the Nest Box

Get a clean bowl and line it with paper towel, paper shreds, or even a washcloth. Lift the babies out of the nest gently and place them in the bowl. Make sure they are firmly down in the bowl - they're squirmy!

Hopefully the nest was lined with a paper towel upon first placing it in the cage, and the Gouldians didn't remove it. This makes it so much easier to clean.

Remove the nest by lifting the paper towel layer under it. It will probably be quite soiled. Toss the towel and bedding. Take the box and scrub if necessary, but usually the mess is contained in the paper towels, so no more cleaning is necessary.

Now re-line the box with clean paper towels, pressing them firmly into the corners. If ants or mites are a problem, sprinkle some diatomaceous earth on the towel. Put in some fresh nesting mix and use your fist to twist/press it down, making a nest shape. Replace the babies and return the nest to its spot.

Fill a small container with nesting material like you did before and give it to the parents, who will probably feel the need to rearrange all that you did.

This is usually done about twice during the nest cycle. The single exclusion is when you smell a strong, pungent odor coming from the box. Not a dirty box smell, but a peculiar one that you never forget. This is an indicator that E. coli has invaded the little family. If this occurs, the box needs to be cleaned ASAP and maybe several times while medicating the hen. With luck, you will be able to save her.

Banding

At age 7-10 days, babies are ready to be banded. Closed bands have to be slipped on over the foot and the hind toe pulled through - so at 8 days they are still small enough to do this without harm. If the bands are split, it doesn't matter when you do it. I put split bands on at 7-8 weeks when I am removing the babies from the parents' flight cage and putting them in their own. I use colors to represent the cock and the hen so that I can keep track of genetics.

Tracking with colored bands means they can be tracked in order to determine their age for breeding purposes, and it gives a quick visual - you'll know not to breed 2 same-color banded birds together.

Finally, They're Out!

Figure 6-3 Fledglings © Patrick Platon.

Baby Gouldians fledge around 23-26 days after hatching. This varies dependent on the climate, conditions of your aviary and the development of the babies. Fledging simply means leaving the nest; they still need to be fed by the parents for about 3 more weeks.

It is a good practice to always catch the first one out and put him back in, one time only. The next day if he is out, leave him; usually there is another adventurous one by this time. Some old-timers believe the one that fledges

THE GOULDIAN FINCH HANDBOOK   147

early will die. Fledglings almost never return to the nest after they have come out.

The following is a loose guide to chick development; all will develop at their own pace.

- At 6 days you should be able to see black feathers appear as stubble.
- At 7 days the eyes open. On day 9, the Gouldian chick has a small tail, and feathers are emerging on the back and wings.
- At about 23 days, the chick will be fully feathered and will fledge (leave the nest).

If a chick is late to fledge, he may remain on the aviary floor for a few days. In this case, lower the highest perch so the parents are closer to him.

Remove the nest box to prevent the parents from abandoning this brood to start a new nest. I have a male that actually switched to a new hen, built a new nest, and left his 3-week-old chicks. There are numerous other stories of Gouldians starting a new nest instead of finishing with the first brood. Protect the ones that are already here rather than trying to bring more into the world.

Weaning

After fledging, the chicks are not weaned -- they still need the parents to feed them.

Soon you may observe the babies picking at seed and pellets, although the parents will continue to feed the chicks after fledging. At about day 31 they should be eating soaked seed, millet, sprouts, and egg food. At this point, provide a small, shallow (not over 1/2") water bowl at the bottom of the cage so the babies can get plenty to drink.

They can leave the cage as early as 35 days old, but it is important to leave them longer with the parents, who can guide them in the ways of being a bird. Chicks that are removed too early can be poor parents (baby tossers) so try to leave the chicks with the parents for a month or more beyond the fledge date. Six weeks would be ideal, longer if at all possible. By that time they are eating well on their own and do not require anything else from the parents. As long as there is no nest and no new chicks coming along, this is perfectly safe.

If one parent or the other begins to molt, they will stop breeding. Do not try to encourage them to continue to breed -- they are simply finished until next year. Continue to provide good food and vitamins to help them grown in a strong, beautiful coat of feathers. Molt is stressful, so keep them together if possible until it is complete.

The first molt from baby colors to adult takes 5 or 6 months *on average.* This is one area where results will vary greatly because it is dependent on environment, genetics, and diet. Molt is a difficult time for finches; this is when it is best to remove the juveniles to a growing-out cage. A regular dose of iodine will help them to reduce stress. Providing stress perches also helps; you can raise many juveniles together, but they still have their private space. Stress perches are perches divided with cardboard, wood or plastic dividers every 5-10 inches. This allows the bird to rest, or perch with one friend, without being hassled by others. You can build your own or purchase them very reasonably online.

The growing-out cage must be kept clean, including floors and perches. Juvies spend a lot of time on the floor. Feed the juveniles with regular seed along with soft food, soaked seed, green food, and a good vitamin.

Problems Regarding Egg Laying

Prolapse

It can be frightening to see a hen with pink tissue hanging out of her back end, known as prolapse. The cloaca is the most common part involved in prolapse, although it could also be the uterus or intestine that the pushing / muscle contraction has expelled.

Prolapse is not limited to egg binding; it also can occur with diarrhea or other illnesses that require the bird to bear down. A veterinarian's care is absolutely required in this life-threatening emergency.

One can find many ideas online for prolapse treatment. Some give incorrect information, and once you've done a particular treatment it cannot be undone. Please read this section through before trying online advice that may or may not be proven, much less accurate.

Keeping the exposed tissue damp is important, and most breeders say a product like KY Jelly or Vaseline lasts a little longer than applying water. Do NOT use Preparation H on a finch! Although it relieves pain and shrinks swelling, it does that in human-size doses, plus it will form a sticky barrier to prevent cleansing; it may even encourage bacteria to grow.

Using a moist Q-tip to push the tissue back in sounds good in theory (one of the suggestions found online) but it is extremely painful for the hen and generally does not work; the tissue will pop back out because a prolapse is more about the muscles contracting to expel the body part, and less about its location. However, if you're like me you want to help at all costs so here's my method for helping a hen with prolapse.

Apply clean table sugar to the tissue to help shrink it. Leave the sugar on for about 20 minutes, then rinse it off. While still moist, wet a Q-tip and gently use it to push the exposed tissue toward the vent. Do not push upward inside the body thinking that you will help it go in further; you will only hurt and possibly injure your bird. If the pressure is successful in moving the tissue inside, hold your finger over the vent for a minute or two before releasing to allow everything to reassemble. The tissue may pop back out; if so, leave it alone and call the vet. In the rare instance, the tissue will stay put. Pat yourself on the back, and return the hen to the hospital cage for a few days.

After a hen has prolapsed, treatment must continue for some time. Prolapse is a symptom of a bigger problem like dietary deficiency, obesity, chronic egg-laying, parasites, or disease. A balanced diet should be first and foremost, with pellets in a larger percentage than seed, as well as calcium-rich fresh foods and/or supplements. Review the vitamin and supplements you've been using, changing brands if necessary or replacing outdated bottles. If egg binding was caused by a deficiency in the diet, Vitamins D3, A, and the all-important calcium are all possibilities. Since it is generally thought that a prolapsed cloaca is brought on by infection, a round of antibiotics is in order. Baytril (the generic is enrofloxyn) is what most veterinarians would prescribe.

Hens with prolapse are likely to experience prolapse again, so do not breed her again right away, if ever. Keeping the hen in a single-sex cage is best. If she is bred, watch carefully for any signs of egg-binding and begin treatment right away. I do not breed hens that have had prolapse - instead they are moved to the Old Birds' cage, where they can live out the rest of their lives.

7 Egg and Baby Problems

Eggs turn beige, clear spot visible - These are most likely infertile eggs. They can be tossed into the trash.

Cracked eggs can occur due to the parents' nails being too long, or other birds entering the nest. Sometimes they can be glued shut and will hatch.

Nestlings dead in shell - Each egg that fails to hatch should be opened for inspection. A dead embryo can be caused by:

- Humidity too low
- Turned wrong in the shell
- Vitamin deficiency
- Bacterial infection
- Poor genes
- Parental inexperience
- Too much temperature variation*

*Temperature variation here refers to the actual temperature of the egg. It isn't your room temperature, but a change caused by the hen not gathering the eggs under

151

her carefully. Providing plenty of nesting material usually will prevent this, as will forming a good nest shape yourself before the birds add to it. Often a too-large nest box is to blame. I had a hen decide to nest in the (dry) bath, which seemed exciting and fun because you could see the nest. Unfortunately she wasn't able to keep the eggs underneath her and all babies died in shell fairly early on. This could have been prevented by adding more nest material around the edges and building up her nest, hindsight being 20/20 and all that.

Chronic Egg Laying

Sometimes a hen lays...and lays...and lays eggs. This can be a sign of a poor diet, notably a fatty one. If that is the case, conversion to a pellet and/or fresh diet will help. Removing nests is another possibility, as is removing the mate or any males that are present. Better yet, move the hen to a larger flight where she can get more exercise.

Reduce daylight hours or cover the cage until she is getting 8 hours of light or less. Hens that are chronic layers will quickly exhaust their calcium supply, so supplements are in order. If feeding a pellet diet, there will already be calcium in the diet so supplementing only every other day or once weekly should be sufficient – check with the vet to be sure.

Egg Binding

Egg binding is an oft-discussed problem for hens. Is it really that common? I think yes, it is. Even an unmated hen can become egg-bound because she is capable of producing eggs when no male is present. It's life-threatening, as the hen only has up to 48 hours to pass the egg or she will die. Fortunately there are a few remedies the owner can use to help her pass the egg. But first, let's see why eggs become bound in the first place.

The egg's yolk is created in the ovary, then passes along the oviduct where the egg white and shell membrane is added. In the uterus, the eggshell is formed. The uterus then contracts to push the egg out the vent.

When egg-bound, the uterus lacks the strength to contract enough to push the egg out. The muscles may be weak due to lack of calcium or other vitamins and/or minerals. The hen may be obese or suffering from infection. The egg could be malformed or simply too large to pass. Some believe there may be a hereditary component.

Your Observations

You may notice her sitting low or straining, pumping the tail up and down ("tail bobbing"). She may pass large or very wet droppings, or none at all. If the egg is pressing on nerves, she may appear to be unable to walk. Gently probing the belly may reveal an egg-shaped object. Sometimes you can see a prolapsed uterus (a reddish part sticking out through the vent). Or you may simply realize things 'aren't right' with your hen. If she has already started laying, the time since the previous egg can be calculated; they usually lay an egg every 24 hours or so.

Treatment

Egg-binding is a life-threatening emergency. Medical treatment that *cannot be done at home* is the best recourse. The veterinarian will give the bird fluids and a combination of antibiotics and calcium. He may also administer steroids or medication to cause her to expel the egg. In some cases the bird needs surgery.

Home Remedies

If you're at home with an egg-bound hen and no avian veterinarian in the area, or it's 2 a.m., you may have no choice but to try to treat it yourself.

The bird should be placed in a hospital cage with very warm temperatures, up to 90 degrees. It is extremely important to raise the humidity in the cage. This could be done by moving the hospital cage to a small bathroom and running the shower to create steam.

Beak dose the hen with electrolytes and calcium every two hours using a pipette. If she won't open, try dripping a small bit on the side of the beak; often you can see her swallowing as it dribbles into her mouth. Many people suggest tapping the beak to get her to open it; I have never managed to do anything with tapping, except maybe get an indignant look from the bird. If you simply cannot administer the mixture, leave it in the water dish as a last resort BUT know that she may not be eating or drinking.

Note: The source of daily calcium should be an avian-specific calcium supplement that also contains vitamin D3. When beak dosing due to egg binding, I would certainly switch to a 23% solution of calcium gluconate along with emergency electrolytes, diluted in water. This product is often available at farm supply stores. I would also put this into her water supply on the off chance that she'd drink some.

Another idea for dosing an egg-bound bird is to give her boiled egg with the shells to eat. It is thought that the calcium obtained from it will help pass the egg.

Many people suggest placing juice from a piece of ginger root directly into her drinking water. I haven't tried this because I haven't had an eggbound hen in years, but

THE GOULDIAN FINCH HANDBOOK   155

it makes sense. Ginger is full of vitamins and may help balance the calcium - phosphorus ratio, and eggs would give her protein for strength. The eggshell, of course, contains calcium and many other minerals, ad the boiled egg gives protein for energy.

If the egg is visible, apply warm water or KY jelly and remove it gently - an egg that breaks inside a hen constitutes a life-threatening emergency, so I can't stress enough how careful one must be. If there appears to be a prolapse (the egg is visible but so is some inner tissue) do not try to remove it; instead get the bird to the veterinarian.

When calcium, heat and humidity have all been applied, warm oil on the vent may help. Since catching her adds stress, this needs to be tried last, after the other remedies.

Related: shell-less or misshapen egg

I was standing in front of a zebra finch cage one evening when a hen got on top of a wicker nest and laid an egg. My mouth dropped open. It was an egg with no shell, exquisitely encased in the membrane. It rolled off the nest and splattered onto the newspaper below before I could close my mouth. Often you don't witness the appearance of shell-less eggs, but might notice a wet yolk on the bottom of the cage or in a nest, absent the shell.

Some causes of no shell or poor shell

- Respiratory disease
- Lack of sunlight
- Too many eggs laid in the season
- Stress (treat with ACV or megamix)
- Genetics
- Insufficient protein
- Overweight

Nestling problems

The crop has air -- this is normal. It should go away on its own. Don't try to squeeze it out, no matter what you read on the Internet; if you bring up food with the air he may aspirate.

The nestling looks dull and wrinkly -- the parents may not be feeding enough. This can be checked by examining the crops in the evenings. If all the chicks look full, they are fine. If they're not, the parents may be ill (does either have a wet vent?) or they could be suffering from loss of nutrition themselves.

A problem that often arises is the parents are only being served hard seed, which they feed to the young but the babies cannot digest it. The solution here is to provide lots of soft egg food and greens to the parents, and perhaps even remove their seed dish during the day if this continues.

The nestling is dark red and shiny - this is a sign of dehydration, often caused by keeping them in a too-warm incubator. It also occurs when people are hand-feeding formula that is too thick. Using a syringe, beak dose a mix of water + pedialyte or bird emergency electrolytes. Repeat until his color is normal and he is defecating regularly. Check the temperature on the brooder to ensure it's not too hot.

Canker

One of the biggest problems with chicks is a protozoon called Trichomonas, or canker. It causes many nestling deaths. If you look in the mouth while the chick begs, you will see white wool-like patches in the mouth, beginning at age 5 days and up. These chicks are weak, and their crops may be empty.

Chicks can be treated for canker with Ronidasole safely. It is a good idea to mix calcium with the medication. Treat for seven days. See the Illness and Treatment chapter for more on canker and it prevention.

Nestling Diarrhea

If the droppings are white and watery, the nest box is wet, and even the feathers are dirty on both the hen and the chicks, the cause is most likely E. coli. It is considered secondary to the cleanliness or dietary problem that brought it on in the first place--clean that cage and all dishes, pronto. In addition, there may be other disease present, like polyomavirus or black spot disease. Nestlings often die between days 5 and 9 if E. coli is present.

Avian polyoma virus (APV) can cause sudden death in 2-3 day old chicks and is particularly prevalent for Gouldian finches. Babies may show hemorrhaging that look like bruising under the skin. It can be carried in birds that do not show signs of infection-- so parents or other birds housed nearby can be carriers.

Determining Color and Sex in Baby Gouldians

One of the down sides of Gouldian ownership is that the babies do not color out for at least three months, and more often it is about eight months before we know what color they will be! However, a sharp owner can compare them in the nest and eventually know what color he or she has before they change.

Here are a few hints for observing colors in the nest.

Upon hatching, Gouldian babies have bright nodules beside their mouths. The outer two are blue and white. The center ones will vary depending on the bird's color. Normal birds and yellow-backed birds have center nodules that are yellow. They may fade to white over time, but for the first ten days or so they are a definite yellow shade.

If the center nodules are white, you know you do not have a green-backed bird. So it will be a blue mutation, which includes blue, pastel blue, and silver. This can be verified by looking at the skin; chicks that are destined to be blue-backed will look a little grayer than its pink nest mates, and chicks that will be yellow are distinctively lighter than the others.

It is said that sexing can be done at fledge, because normal hens will appear grayer than their male counterparts,

and hens have narrower heads. I do not find this to be dependable; to me, colors change, and heads may as well. One breeder suggested never trying to sex the young until after the molt-- a minimum of four months from hatching.

Generally, you will be able to sex the young a couple of months after fledge, when their colors begin to change. Purple breasts in particular are telling, and males will have the distinctive blue, gray, or white pencil line around their masks. The yellow bellies can also be compared, with the male feathers tending toward gold and the female feathers showing more of a lemon yellow. White breasts before molting out are a peculiar shade of brown rather than gray, and in my bloodlines the white breasted birds take longer to molt. If after these markings are examined it still cannot be determined, watch closely for the ones that sing and band those as males.

Weaning

Gouldian chicks can be removed at about 4-5 weeks, but that is not ideal. Instead, be sure that they are eating well on their own. Some breeders wait much longer, feeling that if the parents breed another clutch they should wait until the newest eggs have been hatched out for at least one day, so that the juvenile birds can see the parents feeding the new babies. Since juveniles can injure newly hatched babies, that is not my advice. I wait until about 6-8 weeks to remove them, and during that time I do not give the parents a nest. I toss any eggs they produce; my mantra is "take care of whoever is here first."

Banding baby Gouldians.

There are two kinds of bands: Open and closed. Closed bands are usually aluminum or stainless steel, although you can find some made of plastic. Closed bands are considered a reliable method of identifying a bird, since they cannot be removed at will. They are usually applied at (about) age 8 days. Leg bands can help identify or prove ownership, and they show that a bird is captive bred and not live caught. There is little danger of injury due to a leg band, and keeping your birds in good condition can lower the risks even more.

There are several sources for purchasing closed bands, including the NFSS--National Finch & Softbill Society -- which sells aluminum leg bands that are laser numbered. When you join the society, you will be assigned an I.D.

number that will be printed on each of your bands. There will also be an identification for the individual bird. By banding, you assure buyers that you have a record of where each bird came from and you can provide them with the genetic history of your birds. This is almost a necessity if you are developing a breeding program, because many serious breeders will only purchase close-banded birds. Leg bands can be purchased from a variety of sources listed in the Appendix.

If you are only planning to band with split (color) plastic bands, you can also simply slice children's melty beads (called Perlers) in half with a pill cutter or craft knife, then make a small slit in one side. These are for your own identification purposes only; by selecting a color for each adult and banding the chicks with it, you know which bird is their parent at just a glance. Be sure to sand off any rough edges. If banding in two colors, one can purchase dual color bands, but they offer a limited color range. On the other hand Perlers are found in almost every color at stores like Target and WalMart.

Another more lightweight option is the elastic EZ Rings. I had my doubts about these--the Gouldian size is 0.4 mm smaller than most bands, so on a bigger bird it might be too tight. And if it gets caught on a branch, the finch could hang upside down, unable to free himself. This happened to mine only once, but many people use these without incident. I've ordered two sizes to accommodate bigger legs, and used half regular size and half one size up. They're incredibly easy to put on those little legs, they stay on, and there are no sharp edges to scratch their skin. They're now my favorite band option

When to band

Closed bands like the NFSS bands can be put on between 7-14 days. If applied too early, they fall off in the nest. If applied late, they can be hard to slide onto the foot. I have experienced both ends of this dilemma; one nest full of babies hatched while I was hand-feeding another nest. I thought I knew exactly what day they were born, but they all lost their bands. They must have been younger than I thought.

Another time, I was out of town until day 14. I planned to band on that day, but missed it so I banded on day 15. Two of the babies' legs were already too large for the size D bands I usually use.

Just yesterday, 3 babies that were not over nine days old were too large for size D, but this time I was ready: I had size E on hand. Their nest-mate easily took a size D, and in the next nest over, three babies the same age, 9 days, were about half the size of the first clutch so they too got size D. So you see, banding can be hit-and-miss. It requires watching the eggs to know exactly when they hatched as well as keeping several sizes of bands on hand.

The final method of banding is to purchase your own specially labeled bands (they can be engraved with your own name or business name, plus numbers). These are not terribly expensive, and because they are personalized you can track your own birds fairly easily -- great for those who show, or people who simply 'want to know.' You never know when birds from your aviary might end up in a rescue or other situation that you might need to recover them from.

Split bands or color bands can be applied at any time. Most breeders consider fledgling age the best time to put them on. At this age, they are fairly easy to catch, yet old enough till you will not injure them by putting leg bands on.

Using Band Colors for your Colony

If you are planning to breed your birds on a large scale, you will need a system of identification like I mentioned so that you will not breed within a family. Use split bands or color bands to easily identify breeding pairs and family units. I used to assign a color to every cock and hen, split my bands in half horizontally, and put both colors on the left leg of the babies. At a glance I knew both parents, so I could easily avoid breeding half-siblings to one another. I could also sell a customer an unrelated pair with confidence. I also keep all this in a record book.

Every breeder has his or her own method of using the colored bands. Some people will use the same color for each nest of babies. Some band the parents, then match the babies' bands to the hen's so that they know not to breed back to her with one of those babies. Others put a 'family' color on one leg, and a 'year born' color on the other, then chart all the birds onto a spreadsheet. The system can be as simple or as complicated as you choose.

I personally have a fairly small aviary. I do not always breed finches to the same partner each year. (Note that Gouldians are monogamous, but only for that breeding season. They can be switched to a different mate the following year). So I have assigned every parent bird a leg band color. These days instead of using two bands on the youngsters, I put a family color on. The exception is when the parents switch mates; then I split the bands and babies get 2 colors.

Keeping Records

Because Gouldians look so similar, you may want to create a color-coded system of identifying them with open (split) bands. These are inexpensive and easy to apply.

Here is one simple way of keeping track of your birds. On a computer spreadsheet, make a chart listing the breeding date, parents, their ancestors if known, and the hatch date. A second page can describe each fledgling and their closed band numbers. As they grow, pertinent information can be added: color, fledge date, how long they take to molt out, and to whom they are sold.

Looking back over these records can reveal patterns of behavior, breeding, and possible outcomes of offspring. If the parents' history is not known, the breeding records can help identify recessive traits. This helps not only the breeder but also customers who want to breed their Gouldian finches.

Tips and Ideas about Breeding

Wait until both the male and female are at least one year old before attempting to breed them.

Be prepared for the birds to reject one another. It doesn't happen often, but it does happen.

Breed the Gouldians as close as you can to the same time of year that they hatched. Spend the first year learning the bird's cycle; keep notes and follow that schedule, rather than trying to bend them to your schedule through artificial means. One of the most important items will be when they molt. Some molt in spring and others in fall.

Be aware that outside influences, like weather, can affect the breeding cycle. In Florida after Hurricane

Michael, almost no bird of any species was ready to breed until 2 months or so after the usual time.

In the breeding colony, supply lots of cover in the form of real or fake plants and stress perches for them to sit on. It helps the birds to feel more secure and safe.

Create a system for treatment of mites, protozoa, etc. and utilize it during the month prior to breeding.

Hang nest boxes on the outside of the cage so that you disturb the residents less with nest checking.

Gouldians prefer a half-entrance to a whole entrance to the nest.

Hang feeders on the side of the cage as high as possible rather than setting food on the floor. This is both for sanitary reasons and because they will feel safer eating up high and close to the nest.

Upon hatching, watch closely every day for tossed chicks. Return them to the nest the first time in case it was a clumsy accident. Be prepared for hand feeding (formula and syringe) before it is necessary. Also have a brooder in place to keep babies warm.

Upon hatching, provide egg food to the parents at all times. Dry egg food is fine and does not spoil as quickly as cooked food. (Recipes are in the index for cooked egg food)

Breed only your best birds. Avoid the temptation to breed those carrying a defect that could be genetic. An important but often overlooked genetic defect is baldness.

Leave the young with the parents for 6-8 weeks.

Have a plan for how you are going to keep or sell the young. You might sell them to a pet shop, at a show, or online like Craigslist. But if they don't sell-- then what? If they become full grown, do you have a place to keep them separate from the parents (so they won't breed back to the parents)?

Fast Facts

Eggs laid: 4-8 on average, one each day
Incubation: 15 days
Hatchlings: Remain in nest 21-26 days
Band: 7-9 days
Fledge: 23 Days (about; do not stress or try to help if they do not come out when you expect them to)
Wean: 6 weeks, varies widely
Sexual Maturity: 6 months, but do not attempt to breed until 1 year
Lifespan: 10+ years

Nesting Materials for Gouldian Finches

Coconut Fibers
Cotton bits (natural cotton - never use cotton balls)
Jute or hemp fibers
Burlap threads (cut a piece and pull threads apart)
Paper shreds
Raffia, undyed
Hay
Dried grass, if known to be unsprayed

Offer a variety in a small box or shallow dish. They will choose their favorite, and waste a lot. Nearly every pair is different in their preferred materials as well as the way they construct the nest.

Breeding checklist:

I have between two and five pairs to breed
I have decided whether to breed my birds indoors or outdoors. (Circle one)

I have treated all birds prior to breeding with Ronex, SCATT or S76, and put them on a high protein abundance diet. They have access to cuttle bone or other sources of calcium.

I have ensured that each bird is at least 12 months old (males) or 14 months old (hens). Age two is even better.

I have clipped their toenails so they won't accidentally puncture the eggs.

Incubating and Handfeeding

Incubating eggs

Why would we wish to artificially incubate eggs, instead of leaving them under the Gouldians? There are many good reasons. Often young parent birds don't sit on the eggs, or aren't sitting tight enough; the temperature change can cause eggs not to hatch. Sometimes the hen passes away during incubation. Some people want to have a chance to enjoy the entire process from the beginning.

For the best results in incubating eggs, everything must be precise. The temperature, humidity and how often the eggs are rotated all must be regulated. Parent birds turn eggs an average of once every 1/2 hour, so we want to emulate that as best we can. Every hour is optimal, but they can be successfully hatched by turning once every three to four hours.

Steps for Preparation:

Purchase a commercial incubator
Run it for a week to stabilize temperature and work out the humidity requirements

Ideal temperature is 95 degrees (35 C) with 60% humidity

An incubator of sorts can be created from a glass aquarium and a ceramic heat lamp or even a heating pad. I find that a true incubator is fairly inexpensive and provides a more stable temperature than the homemade variety. This link http://goo.gl/qV9FmP shows the type of incubator I am currently using. I did not opt for the egg turner, because I leave the eggs under the hens. My incubator is mainly used as a brooder for chicks that have already hatched.

Good hygiene is a MUST. Wet hands can remove the egg's natural protection, and germs can be transferred via the permeable shell. Besides washing hands, it is best to slip on some disposable gloves each time the eggs will be handled.

When you begin incubating eggs, turn them seven times per day. For multiple eggs, mark one side with an X and the other with an O. Use a pencil, not an alcohol marker. By keeping track of which letter is showing you will know whether you have turned them all or not.

On day 15 or 16, you may notice the chick rotating in the egg, cutting a thin line. Do not rotate. Do not help him. Assisting weakens him - it does a lot of harm. Hatching can take hours. After he hatches, keep him in a warm spot and don't handle him too much. Let him rest for about a day, maybe even two. At that point he will absorb the yolk sac and start begging to be fed. Now the fun begins!

Hand Feeding

When breeding Gouldian finches, sooner or later you will have to hand feed one. Many occurrences can lead to this: a parent dies, the parents lack experience, they become exhausted from a large brood, or the really ugly one -- they toss the chicks. Sometimes one chick lags behind the others, so you elect to hand feed it.

There is definitely an art to hand feeding birds, and it would be best to learn all you can *before* the time arrives--because it's an emergency once it does. The best way, of course, is to find a mentor and see how to feed in person. Whether or not a mentor is available, if finches are breeding one must stock up on feeding tools and supplies, including finch formula, read through this guide and perhaps watch a video or two. Anyone who breeds their birds on purpose should have a plan for hand-raising hatchlings.

Supplies (see Appendix and the website)

- Thermometer
- Formula – Roudybush, Kaytee Exact
- Toothpick
- Syringe, dropper, or pipette for feeding
- Pedialyte, Megamix, ER Formula, Vitalize, or NV Powder (see supplements, below)
- Small nest
- Gram scale

The simplest solution for tossed or abandoned babies is to use foster parents. Please see the next section for more information on fostering. In this section we will discuss hand feeding and hand rearing the babies yourself.

I will offer up one word of caution: hand rearing baby birds is WORK. I was with friends once when we came upon a pet store whose owner purchases one-week-old chicks, including Lady Gouldian finches, and hand-rears them to sell in the shop. "You should do that," someone said to me.

THE GOULDIAN FINCH HANDBOOK   169

I knew this would never be the case. Pulling a baby to simply make it 'tame' is dangerous to its health. There are no guarantees-- chances are less than 50% that the chick will survive to adulthood. In the meantime, you are giving up your entire life (I'm not exaggerating) to feed them.

Most people have no idea what it's like on the 5th or 7th day of feeding every hour and a half to two hours around the clock. Exhaustion sets in, but still the finch needs to be fed. Plus, feeding such a tiny baby means he may breathe the food into his lungs (aspirate). He could catch a virus. He might not digest the formula well. He may simply fail to thrive.

Worse, when you return a hand-raised baby to the aviary, it doesn't necessarily remain tame. It could revert to the wild behavior of its cage mates, fearing you because the other birds do.

However, accidents and mishaps cause us to need to raise babies by hand, so I will do my best to explain my method of doing it. I will say that the first time I was faced with a 9-day-old chick to raise, I followed directions -- to the letter--that I found on the Internet. The baby died. I then purchased a book to use as guidance, but by the time it arrived I was following yet another website's guidelines. The two sites were completely different, and the advice from the book was different than what the websites suggested. Now I am adding a fourth protocol to the mix. Which one is right? The one that works for you. All I can tell you is this is what I have done and it works.

Kaytee Exact Handfeeding Formula is available nationwide at most big box pet stores, and it works fine. You will need small measuring spoons to measure out the formula, and both a toothpick and a syringe for feeding. It is advisable to add one drop of Megamix or applesauce to the formula each time you feed it. If the babies are tiny, it is helpful to get an extension for the syringe, either a crop tube or a teat. The teat is not flexible like a crop feeding tube, but it helps direct the food into the back of those tiny mouths.

For the makeshift nest, some people bunch up a towel or paper towels. Some spread soft litter-like material on the floor of the incubator. I use a canary nest and place paper towels in it that can be changed each time the bird soils it. The towels are necessary to keep chicks from catching toenails on the nest threads.

Day 1

You find a hatchling that has been abandoned. It is cold but still alive. Put the baby back in with the parents at least once or twice. Inexperienced birds are especially apt to toss their babies. To them, strange little mutants have shown up in the nest! Occasionally I think it's simply an accident that the baby got pushed out. Sometimes they will begin caring for the babies after the second attempt. It is good to try this about one hour before they go to nest; this seems like a calmer time of day when they are more accepting.

If your efforts do not work, it is time to begin caring for your new baby. Hopefully you set up the brooder and turned it on as soon as you found the tossed chick(s). Set the temperature at 94-96 degrees and heat it up, checking fairly often to be sure the temperature doesn't fluctuate. Fill the humidity trays, or determine another way to provide moist air to the chick.

Most sources claim it is not necessary to feed the chicks the first day or two because the yolk sac hasn't been absorbed yet. But it's really hard to keep them alive, especially if they've been tossed and gotten cold.

THE GOULDIAN FINCH HANDBOOK   171

I have even had chicks that did not show the yolk sac on what I believed to be the first day. Here is what I think happened: Even though I was checking the nest daily, they may have hatched after the nest check the day before, or they may have absorbed the yolk more quickly because they were tossed and became cold. Whatever the reason, I did go ahead and begin feeding on Day 1 (despite all that well-meant advice from others). It was the right decision; they were hungry!

So if it is within the first 24-48 hours and you have determined it is right to feed the baby, wash your hands, get a flat toothpick and mix up a tiny amount of watery formula. Even a teaspoon full is too much for a single baby. Use half water and half pedialyte to give him a boost, with only a small bit of formula mixed in. The temperature of the formula should be in the mid to high 90s. Too hot and it scalds the bird's mouth, which will be fatal. Too cold and he will not be able to digest it properly. Set the formula in a bowl of hot water and let it rest a few minutes so that the powder gets completely saturated. It may be necessary to add more water.

I like to sand my toothpick on all sides, especially the end, to be sure it will not harm the baby's mouth. Wait until he opens his mouth to beg for food. If he's not begging, stroke his back or touch his beak. Use the toothpick to dip small bits of formula and place it in the baby's mouth.

Now for the most important part of the hand-feeding process: getting into position. If you want, hold the head up and keep it still by grasping it between two fingers and hold the feeding tool at the left of the baby's beak. Wait until he begs and put the food into his mouth.

Let him rest between bites. He will only take a few mouthfuls every hour or hour and one half. When he stops begging, don't try to force feed. Wipe his mouth, change the towels in the nest, and place him back in the brooder immediately, so he won't chill. This is not the time to begin trying to bond (that can come later). Wash your hands again.

Every time you feed, follow the same procedure: Wash your hands thoroughly with anti-bacterial soap, heat the water, use a thermometer to test the water temperature, and mix the formula. Fill a clean, sterilized syringe (or sterilize the toothpick if the baby is under 48 hours old). To keep the temperature up in the syringe, place it in a bowl of hot water.

Things to remember:

- Mixing with pedialyte in the first days is advisable (it gives the baby electrolytes). I usually alternate between pedialyte and water.
- Let the formula rest before feeding. If the formula is too thick, the bird will be unable to digest it. Keep it thin.
- Do not save mixed formula beyond two or three hours. It is safe to refrigerate it for that period of time and reheat it, but do not store it any longer -- it ruins in no time.
- Add a drop of Megamix or unsweetened applesauce to each feeding to fight yeast infections.
- Sterilize everything between feedings, and keep your hands clean especially if you have other birds.
- Feed whenever the crop empties – 3 or 4 times during the night and about every 2 hours during the day.

Day 2

If you have made it 24 hours, congratulate yourself on a job well done. Hand rearing is tedious and difficult – but

THE GOULDIAN FINCH HANDBOOK 173

I promise it gets easier. You'll notice that the baby begins to outgrow its toothpick-sized feedings, so it is time on Day 2 or 3 to switch up to a crop tube or pipette. You will see that the end of a syringe, even 1cc size, is too large and difficult to use. Pipettes are easier and a little more forgiving if you bump that tiny mouth. A crop tube or teat, even if you just put it in the mouth and don't try to push it down into the crop, is the perfect size.

Using a syringe, suck the food up and hold it tip-up, letting all the air rise to the top. Push out the air until a little formula mixture comes out before you begin to feed. Point the syringe toward his right so that the food can enter the crop and not the lungs. Wait until the baby is begging before attempting to feed it; the begging motion means it has closed off the airway, so it will not aspirate.

Press the end of the syringe very slowly to allow only a seed-size drop at a time. After it swallows, let the chick work on the food before trying to offer more. Sometimes they need a long break.

Feed the baby as often as you can -- every time he is begging, but only if he is begging. Do not try to feed when he's not asking; you can cause him to aspirate. Wipe the beak between servings. If he will lay on his back, this gives you a good angle for feeding him If there is no more begging do not force him to eat. This will get easier as both you and the baby learn to coordinate the efforts.

Continue to monitor the temperature in the brooder. Weigh the baby daily and feed about 10% of his weight.

You can also gavage (tube) feed your babies although I do not recommend it. The tube fits on the end of a syringe and is pushed down into the crop to feed directly into it instead of into the mouth first and then the crop. it is a faster way to feed the babies. However, birds can suffer from stress or injury by tube feeding. Additionally there's no way of knowing whether the baby wants to eat or not; you're simply stuffing the food in. This could cause the crop to stretch or rupture.

To feed a clutch, place the babies in a small plastic container – an empty margarine tub is perfect. Line it with tissues before you begin, or just pop the entire nest into the tub. Set up a heat source, either a lamp or a ceramic reptile heater, so the babies' body temperature will not drop while you are feeding. Use a separate syringe for each chick so as not to pass disease.

	Age of Chick	Stage
90-94 F / 32.2 - 34.4 C	0-3 days	Newly hatched
88-92 F / 31.1 – 33.3 C	4-6 days	Still not feathered
85-89 F / 29.4 – 31.6 C	6-9 days	Pin feathers
82-86 F / 27.7 – 30 C	10-12 days	Small tail is formed
Room temperature	18-23 days	Fully Feathered

Supplements

There are more supplement ideas for hand-feeding than there are Gouldians in the world, I suspect. I have heard of people adding powdered milk, multi-vitamins, applesauce, baby cereal, and many more additives. My opinion is that except for applesauce and apple cider vinegar, they are fairly unproven so it would be best to avoid them. Instead, select a good quality formula made especially for hand-feeding and feed it to your birds. When they are older, you can make nutritional adjustments as you see fit. Right now, our only goal is to keep the baby birds alive.

Hand feeding problems

The bird will not open its beak.

Sometimes the bird will respond to a light tap on the beak with the syringe. Other times you can dribble a tiny bit of formula on the upper left side; this will dribble down into the lower beak and he usually will open his mouth. You can also use your hand to create a 'shadow' across his head; sometimes that will encourage them to open wide.

I don't think the bird ate enough.

The general rule with hand-feeding parrots is they eat 10% of their body weight. Think about that in relation to your newborn finch. Use the scale to weight him - finches are tiny! Most of the time they will eat as much as they need. .1 or .2 cc may be all they want. Do not force it to overeat, but do offer food around the clock every two hours.

It's been well over 2 hours and the crop hasn't emptied.

It's okay if the crop only empties every 24 hours, but here are some reasons the food may not be moving. The food may be too dry; it should have the consistency of creamed soup. Later it should be as thick as heavy cream. There is information floating around on the Internet that formula should have the consistency of pudding. For Americans, this is going to result in a thick mess that your finch can't digest and your syringe cannot take up. Best to make it like creamy soup, and err on the side of caution: making it too watery simply means you will feed a little more often. Too thick can cause bigger, possibly fatal problems.

Sometimes the food temperature is too cold, and it will sit in the crop and not move. If the crop is overfilled, the food may not move. If the crop is stretched by overfeeding or scalded by too-hot food, it will remain still. Suctioning the food back out of the crop is risky and dangerous, but it may be an only option if the food has remained for more than 24 hours. Some veterinarians suggest giving the finch water or watery applesauce, wait a bit, and then suction it out.

The crop has air.

Air in the crop is generally normal. Do not worry about it.

That said, there is one instance in which crop air is a worry, and that is when yeast infection is building up air in the crop. You will see it expand even though you haven't fed in awhile, and there may be a bit of food still in the crop. To resolve this, put some Megamix or applesauce into the formula; the acidity will offset the yeast. Apple cider vinegar, just a tiny amount, may also be used.

Nestlings are dull and /or wrinkly

They aren't getting enough food or water. Do not ever strictly follow package guidelines for hand-feeding; instead, watch for signals from your babies. There will be times when you have to feed them every hour instead of every two; or they were up to 3-hour intervals and suddenly you're back at it in one and a half hours. All normal; these changes indicate growth spurts. They're for celebration, even if by now you are sorely sleep deprived!

If the babies' skin is shiny and red, the incubator is too hot or the babies are dehydrated. Remember to check the humidity, adding a humidifier if necessary.

Why parent birds toss babies

Most people claim it is the male that throws the babies from the nest upon hatching. However, I had a hen that would grab them by the head or wing, go as far as she could get from the nest, and fling away the babies. Why?

Some say the male is reverting to courtship stages; raising babies isn't where his mind is at the moment. Sometimes the parents, or one of them, may be too new to this. They may do fine with the next batch. Often they will toss babies because of stress, usually from too much human interference in the nesting stage. You can remedy this by leaving them alone –no more nest checks whatsoever, and covering the half of the cage where the nest is with cardboard or fabric.

Also, the birds can have so much nutrition in the form of rich, soft food that they are overly energized. Try reducing or eliminating the soft food supply between the date they lay the eggs and the hatch date. They will need to utilize soft food while they're feeding young, so be sure to start it back.

Because Gouldians are notorious for not being good parents, I knew going into this that I wanted mine to be the best parents possible. To that end, I refuse to breed any bird that tossed babies. Fortunately, putting the babies back worked with the first few, and after that I learned that breeding young birds was part of the problem. Now I have solid parent birds that take good care of the babies, and I can't tell you how long it's been since we found one on the floor.

Hand Taming Finches

It is rare, but not unheard of to see hand-tamed Gouldians. It is possible to tame them, and those that are hand-fed will sometimes remain tame, but if returned to the aviary they can quickly revert to the wild behavior of their flock. We had a blue-back once that had to be medicated for about 6 of his first 12 weeks of life. He remained calm when we reached into the cage, and was willing to be handled long after returning to his flock.

Finch wranglers I know have said "just handle them a lot," and they must be pulled from the nest at 10 days to be properly imprinted on a human. Because there is a high risk of losing nestlings at that age, I personally will not do it. Also, one that is tame cannot ever go back to the colony successfully; he doesn't know he's one of them. So a person would have to be prepared to be "bonded" to a finch for 10 years or more, or rehome it.

If you're dead set on hand taming, prepare for hand-feeding as described above. You'll need a brooder of some sort to keep the baby in. Pulling the finch at 10 days means you'll have to feed him for the next 25 days without fail; how is that going to fit with family, work, and vacations?

Many birds are "hand raised" meaning that they are hand *fed* but not necessarily hand *tame*. To truly tame your finch, don't just feed him and put him away. Spend plenty of time holding him, talking to him, and wearing him in your collar or pocket. Place a small perch near your sofa or desk. Offer a treat like short bits of millet from your hand as soon as he's able to eat it; this way he'll learn that flying to you gets him a treat.

Societies as Fosters

Because Gouldians are not the world's greatest birdie parents, people turn to other types of birds to raise the chicks. Many people keep a few Society Finches on hand for this purpose, although zebra finches or even other Gouldians can often do it. Societies are particularly good foster parents for Gouldians. They don't have to be a male-female pair; sometimes three males or a pair of hens will take over the parenting and do a great job. If you are already familiar with your Societies as parents, choose the tighter sitters for your foster parents.

Society finches in this case do best in a cage with only a few birds rather than a mixed colony. This is because they are so social. Colony life can be distracting for such social birds. Set them up as pairs or in a small 2-nest cage of three or four birds. Use caution; I once had a cage of 8, and they had three nests with clear nest "owners." Yet every time I put Gouldian eggs in one nest, everybody went into that one and sat on them -- and broke them. If this happens, split them up into smaller groups.

Societies used for fostering should be in a nesting cycle before handing off chicks to them if at all possible. Sometimes they will incubate a clutch of eggs properly without it, but to have the best success I would breed them at the same time as the others, or, if that is not possible, give them some dummy eggs. If they begin to sit on the dummy eggs, you can switch those out with real eggs should the need arise.

People who become really serious about fostering Gouldians, perhaps so that they can produce the largest number possible, use 3 pairs of foster Societies for every pair of Gouldian birds. All the birds will work hard for 9 months and rest for 3. In other words they have about

6 rounds of 4-6 eggs at a time from the Gouldian pairs, and they'll usually start laying again in 6 weeks so that's 9 months-- and if they're healthy and a little luck is involved, they have 210 babies for every cycle.

A 5-inch long plastic nest box works best for human nest-check purposes, although most Societies take readily to a wicker nest. With the Bengalese or Society Finches, give them a nest box and keep checking it until they have laid their first egg. About 2 days later when they lay their 3rd egg, remove their three eggs and replace them with Gouldian eggs. This is simple math; Society Finches sit on eggs for 14 days, but Gouldians don't hatch until the 16th day so we're sort of manipulating the process. The Society Finch would usually lay a couple more eggs, and you absolutely must remove these or they might feed their own and not feed the foster babies.

How in the world will you identify those eggs? Hopefully you marked the Gouldian eggs before you put them in the nest, so the unmarked eggs will be the ones belonging to the Society Finches.

By now you've figured out how many cages are required to practice this process, and you've probably noticed that the weaned Gouldians will need a growing-out cage also. You might be thinking this isn't even fun. You're right, and my personal opinion is that we'd be better off to breed birds that are healthy and able to raise their own. On the other hand, if the Europeans had not used fosters to work with the Gouldian stock they had, we probably wouldn't even have any Gouldians in captivity now.

It is a myth that Society Finches should never raise their own babies. This is touted as the reason they will reject other babies; however, if the birds are mature and have had a clutch of their own, they seem accepting of other babies, even those that don't "look like" their own young (Gouldians have the distinct mouth markings, for example). In fact, the parenting instinct is usually so strong with Society Finches that they will take on a new hatchling even with a nest of ready-to-fledge youngsters. Not recommended -- but possible!

Some breeders keep the same number of Society Finch pairs as Gouldian pairs. As soon as an egg is laid, they move it to the corresponding society nest. For them, the system works well, resulting in healthy, beautiful Gouldians.

Problems with fostering

Contrary to popular belief, not all Society Finches make good parents. Fostering is a process that must be closely watched and examined. Also, any Societies to be used as fosters should have a healthy diet full of protein prior to the appearance of any eggs.

Age matters. Society Finches must be sexually mature, or they will not incubate, feed, or care for babies.

Societies might not incubate small clutches, so putting fewer than four eggs in their nest is risky. Add plastic eggs if necessary.

There is always a chance of disease. Some viruses come in a wave occasionally just like the flu virus does. If this happens, eggs from the diseased birds can be fostered under disease-free parents that are kept separately, and hopefully they will hatch. Society finches can be carriers of both campylobacter and cochlasoma. They're considered silent carriers; that is, they do not have the active infection, but they carry the disease in their bodies and it will infect any bird that isn't already immune to it. Society finches have good immune systems and can carry a low-level bacterial or parasite infection without compromising their own health -- thought it will affect their productivity over time.

They're able to raise their own young, but when given Gouldians to foster, the Gouldians always die. People refer to this as "Bengalese disease."

Both of these diseases, though, can be held in remission during breeding season. This is done through a treatment protocol just before breeding. Erythromycin is the drug of choice for treating campylobacter, though some use doxycycline or tetracycline. Since neither of these last two are recommended for chicks, the erythromycin is the better choice.

Cochlasoma is the one disease that might be hard to treat, and it can only be diagnosed by a vet. To apply a treatment for Cochlasoma before fostering, breeders suggest dosing with Ronidazole 12% at a rate of 1.5 teaspoons per gallon of water. This will need to be done every other week thereafter until the chicks are weaned.

There is one huge drawback to this method. If we give the medication to the Societies, we are also medicating the chicks. This could lead to a weakened immune system in the babies – and as breeders, we must be responsible and only breed the best, strongest finches we can produce. A better plan might be if chicks are lost with a certain pair of Societies, assume they are carriers and remove them from the breeding program.

Mixed Species Nests

By mixing Gouldians with Societies, the way they are fed is somewhat altered. If the Societies hatch their own young alongside the fosters, the Gouldians may also be ignored a bit because the parents favor their own young. Another problem occurs when babies fledge at different ages. Sometimes the parents wean the older babies (the Society Finches) and stop feeding the younger ones (the

Gouldians), which aren't ready to stop eating yet. These babies will starve to death unless they are hand-fed to weaning.

That said, the Gouldian chicks may catch up growth-wise once they reach the age of three months or so.

Imprinting

Gouldians will imprint on the Society Finches, since they imprint on whomever is raising them. To help them be more Gouldian-like, simply remove them as soon as they are independent, around 40 to 45 days after hatching, and put them with some Gouldians. This way they will not reject Gouldians later on--and they will learn more Gouldian-like songs.

Gouldians that are not allowed to raise their own young may become reluctant to breed. Over a few generations, this causes fertility to drop in the line. You may find that pairs will no longer raise their own young at all. Sometimes the females lay tons of eggs, many of them infertile, and die young because of some disease or simply exhaustion from over breeding.

Usually if you revert back to non-fostering, some will self-rear, but it won't be even half. They will scatter the nesting material you've placed in the nest box, or the female lays eggs on the bare nest box floor or even the bare cage floor. Males lack interest in breeding. If you are intent on creating good parents, keep working with the same birds and keep some of the youngsters (from the self-rearing parents only) and continue breeding, and in a few years they will again be a self-rearing colony. This is the *only* time I recommend breeding non-rearing parents. I do not use society finches for fostering at all. I believe we need to encourage natural behavior, including parents raising their own young. If a parent bird will not raise babies, I remove it from the breeding program.

One positive reason to use Societies as fosters is that Societies are a lot more willing to eat a varied diet, and more likely to try new foods. I find if I introduce new food in my aviary, the Societies are first to go to it, but the entire flock reacts by following their example. Hence, I can make sure babies are eating a varied diet even if the (original) parents were not.

Another good reason to foster is if you're line-breeding, and you want to be sure to get some progeny from a particular pair. The fosters can help make it easier to ensure your success.

Some breeders believe that Society color makes a difference – that the darker ones, for example, will be more likely to raise darker babies. As with everything, test your own theories and do what works best for you and your aviary.

8   Does That Come in Pink? Genetics

This book would not be complete without a discussion of colors and how they come about. I am not a scientist, and this is merely my understanding of how Gouldian genetics work. There are slight disagreements even among experts about the heredity of some colors—some insist there is another species involved. The terminology has not been standardized either, making a a genetics discussion even more confusing. I'll try my best to make it clear.

A "normal" Gouldian finch has a green back, red head, purple breast, and yellow belly. If it is a cock it has those colors and a pearly white beak with a red tip. The normal hen's coloration is softer than the male's. If she is in breeding condition, her beak will turn black.

Besides the normal colorations, there are a few others which are called mutations. These can show up naturally, but often people develop mutations by selective breeding.

DNA is what determines coloration in any animal. In order to understand how color works in the Gouldian finch, we must first know a little bit about genetics. I'll give a brief overview as a reminder.

Genetic Terminology

We all know there are genes that determine our finch's makeup. Those genes are responsible for putting together everything about the bird, including its sex and colors. Colors can be dictated by different forms of a gene, called alleles. In the Gouldian finch's back color, for example, there are alleles for green, blue, and yellow. An allele can be dominant or recessive. If it is dominant, you will know right away because *in general* you will see more of that color in nature.

The chromosomes have alleles containing the genetic material, which are always present in pairs. These pairs will either be sex chromosomes or non-sex ones, which we call autosomes. The sex chromosomes will determine the sex of the bird. Whereas mammals are described in X and Y, we denote a cock with "Z" (ZZ) and a hen with W (She carries two, so ZW). You might recall that in mammals, males were XY and females XX, so Gouldian sex chromosomes are reversed. Only the Z carries color information; the W makes the bird a hen but does not carry color. So when we describe a color as sex-linked, we mean it is carried by the Z chromosome.

Genetic charts are used to illustrate the genetic makeup of parent birds, along with the possible outcomes in the young. For example, we breed a normal (green-backed) male to a normal hen. The results can be shown visually in a Punnett's Square:

Cock: ZZ (Z is denoted by green)
Hen: ZW (W is denoted by white)

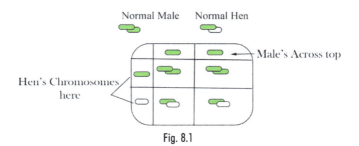

Fig. 8.1

By crossing each pair of chromosomes, we see all the resulting possible combinations of birds -- 50% males (ZZ) AND 50% Females (ZW).

From the chart, we can expect all offspring to have green backs. The W denotes a hen, so about 50% of the offspring are expected to be hens.

Now let's examine how birds carry genes. "Locus" (Plural: loci) is the word we use to indicate a genetic location. The word location can help remember it.

Autosomal means that the gene in question is located on one of the non-sex chromosomes. Both cocks and hens can carry them. Their loci may contain identical genes, which would make the bird's color a "double factor", or they may contain different genes. If the locus is for chest, and a bird carries both purple and white, we say it is visually purple but 'split' for white. That's because purple is dominant. (We'll discuss that further on.) If a bird is split, we have no way of knowing what it is split for unless we breed the bird and see a result.

So in order to determine what color your bird's offspring might be, you need to know what colors sex-linked, what colors are represented, and how they present themselves.

Head Colors

Lady Gouldians come in three head colors: red, yellow, and black. We abbreviate them RH, YH, and BH. A yellow head is visually orange. In scientific terms, the *phenotype* is what we see (orange head) and the *genotype* is the actual genetic makeup (yellow pigment, although this is oversimplification).

Note that hens that are not black headed often have a lot of black feathering in their head coloration, which is not a fault but simply part of their coloration. We still refer to them by the color we see there, i.e. red or yellow. If a hen has an excess of dark feathering, she's sometimes referred to as a dirty red head or yellow head.

Red Head (RH) is sex-linked dominant. That means a cock can be double factor for the red head, or single factor (he will express the red, but carry another color). A hen can only be single factor (SF). Neither will ever be 'split' for Red head.

The Black head is a sex-linked recessive trait. Cocks can be double factor (show a black head) or single factor (split for black head). A hen will only be single factor. She will never be 'split' for black head.

Let's look at a pair of Gouldian finches, a red-headed male, and a black headed female. Here is what the chart would look like for head color, if the male carried two chromosomes for red head:

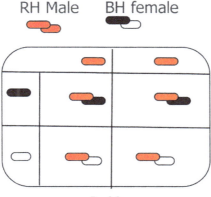

Fig. 8.2

Remember that hens carry the W as their second chromosome. So we see that all the male offspring will be red-headed males *split to black* (they carry a gene for black heads), and all the hens will be red headed. Hens are not split; they carry only one chromosome, and it's red.

Let us now take one of the red-headed split to black cock babies and breed him with a black-headed female.

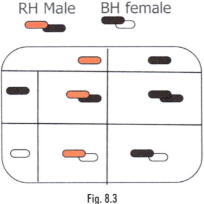

Fig. 8.3

Now in theory we will have 50% of the male babies red-headed and 50% black headed. The hens will also be 50% red headed and 50% black headed.

Yellow head seems to be the head color that's most confusing. Yellow (visual orange) is an autosomal recessive trait. *It requires at least one red head gene in order to be expressed.*

"But wait – didn't you say red was dominant?"

Yes, red is dominant. But the yellow pigment suppresses the ability to show red. So yellow shows up if (1) there are 2 copies of the yellow allele and (2) there's red present.

Many people feel that yellow is "separate" from red and the two should not be mingled. But without the red gene, what would happen?

If two yellow head genes are present, but a bird does not have red head genes (meaning it has black head genes) it will have a black head. So if you're breeding for yellow head, don't be afraid to allow red headed birds into the mix.

The black headed bird with two yellow head genes will be immediately evident. We know it carries yellow head because its beak is tipped with yellow. This bird is genetically yellow headed, but the yellow depends on the red gene for expression—and there's no red gene present.

Cocks and hens both may be split for yellow head. The accompanying yellow-tipped beak is usually abbreviated YTB.

Breast Color

Lady Gouldians can have one of three recognized breast colors: purple, lilac, and white.

A purple breast is autosomal dominant, so both cocks and hens can be a double factor or single factor purple breast. They will express it if they have it, and it is present in combination with all head/ body colors. No Gouldian will ever be split for purple breast. Purple breast presents as a deep royal purple in cocks and paler purple or rose in hens.

Figure 8-4 Male (left) Female (right)

Lilac breast is an autosomal trait that is recessive to purple but dominant to white. To have a lilac breast, a bird must be double factor for lilac, or single factor for lilac and split to white. If a bird is single factor for lilac and also for purple, it will be visually purple breasted and split to lilac (Purple/lilac). Lilac breast can be expressed alongside every head and body color except pastel cock body colors, which are caused by the purple breast. Lilac color can vary, ranging from very pale purple, like that in a normal hen, to a deep purple approaching that of a purple-breasted normal male.

White breast is recessive. Cocks and hens can be double factor and express a white breast, or they will be split to white while showing another color (purple or lilac). White breasted birds cannot be split to another color. The white breast can occur with every head and back color except the pastel body colors. If a bird is truly white breasted, you will see pure white. If it has flecks of purple, it is a "bad white breasted" bird.

It is not possible for a Gouldian to carry all three of the alleles. Because there are only two copies of the breast color gene present in the genome, a Gouldian will carry only two alleles.

What does this mean? If you breed a purple breasted cock that carries two purple genes to a bird carrying another color, you will get purple breasted birds that are split for white or lilac breast. Breeding two purple breasts together, if they both carry 2 purple genes, will result in all purple. The fun happens because we don't always know what our birds are split for. So we breed two purples together, but because each carried a white gene (both birds are split to white) we get a white breasted baby. This will only occur a small percent of the time. Here is how we would chart that breeding:

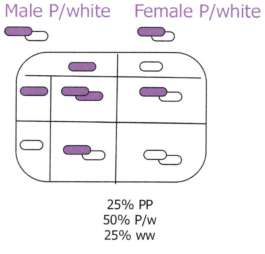

Fig. 8.5

25% of the offspring are double factor purple breasts. (PP, or DFPB)

50% have purple breasts, but are split to white (SFPB, or Purple/white). You do not have a way of knowing which ones are which; splits are not visual, they are located in the genes. 25% of the babies have turned up with white breasts, DFWB. You are left wondering where the white came from.

Note that this is a statistics-based chart. That means if you have 4 young in the nest, the genes *most likely* will occur in this scenario. However, it is entirely possible to breed the same pair repeatedly and only occasionally have the white breast show up. It is akin to flipping a coin; over time, if we toss the coin enough, we will approach the statistical average we expect. In the short term, though, we could toss a coin ten times and get any combination of results--even a solid run of heads, or in this case, purple breasts.

Body Color Genetics

There are many mutations of Gouldian body colors, and some still being developed. There are bound to be many more in the future. Here are some: Sea green, European Yellow, Australian Yellow, White-Headed/White-breasted, Pastel, Silver.

In the U.S., there are fewer colors normally available. Let's focus on those for our genetics discussion.

Gouldian hens only come in four body colors, while cocks have six. Here they are:

Hens: green, yellow, blue, silver. Hens can also be pastel, but because it's a hen the pastel is visually yellow.

Cocks: green, pastel (soft green, in the US we tend to use the slang term dilute), yellow, blue, pastel blue, silver.

The body color can affect the head colors; the yellow body color gene suppresses black head color, causing it to be white in appearance. The blue body color gene suppresses the expression of red and yellow, so the head on these birds will appear as tan or straw color.

Figure 8-6 Body colors

Green body is incompletely dominant to yellow. Green is dominant to blue. So cocks can be double factor or single factor for green. Hens can only be single factor for green--remember that 'w' they carry.

Fig 8.7 Single Factor Green Back
© Tina Billings 2020

Pastel green is a special shade when yellow and green are both present in a male purple breasted bird. These are commonly referred to as "dilutes" although the proper term is pastel. Pastel greens have a brighter green back coloration, and they are always males. The color of pastel green is like you took your green and yellow crayons and colored the bird; he is soft green, sort of a combination of both. And that is a great visual example of incomplete dominance. You will never have a pastel green hen because both green and yellow chromosomes are required to create it, and the hens only have a single color gene.

Pastel green does not occur in white breasted cocks, but pastel birds may be split for white breast.

Yellow body is sex-linked and incompletely dominant to green. It is dominant to blue body. Cocks can be double factor (DF) or single factor (SF) for yellow. Hens are only single factor. Yellow body occurs in combination with any head or breast color. A cock that is single factor for yellow and has a purple chest appears darker in tone and the pencil line around his neck is either gray or bluish in color. If he carries green and yellow (SF yellow) with a white or lilac chest, he appears yellow. The yellow gene suppresses the expression of black, so anything that would normally be black appears white, or sometimes off-white. That's why yellow birds with black heads appear to have gray or white heads. For a double factor yellow cock, the pencil line around the neck is white.

Fig. 8.8 Single Factor Yellow Back © Tina Billings 2020

Blue body--be still, my heart! -- is an autosomal recessive gene. Both cocks and hens can be double factor and express blue, or single factor and split for blue. Birds are only visually blue when the sex chromosome carries green, not yellow. Blue can occur in combination with any head or breast color, but blue suppresses both red and yellow. So a red or yellow headed blue-back will have a tan or salmon-colored head and an off-white belly. The black head remains black.

Pastel blue is a blue-bodied bird carrying a copy of the yellow gene. The slang terms for pastel blue include silver, dilute blue, and powder blue, but all are pastel. Hens appear silver. White-breasted males appear silver. Purple-breasted males appear powder blue.

Let's take a green-backed male split to blue and a green hen. Will we get any blue?

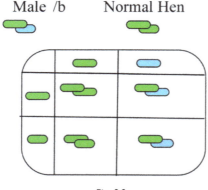

Fig. 8.9

25% Green-backed males, 50% green/b, 25% green-backed hens.

The results show that half the offspring will be split to blue, with no visual indicator. There are no visual blue-backed birds.

What if the cock and hen are both split to blue? Does this feel like a trick question? This is not a sex-linked characteristic -- so indeed they can both be split to blue. The nest will contain about 25% green-backed birds with no split, 50% showing green but split to blue, and 25% blue-backed hens. But remember the coin-tossing game – results may vary.

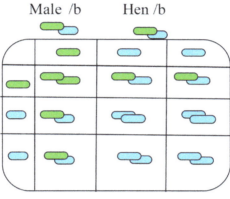

Fig. 8.10

Ino Colors

There is an interesting and (in the United States at least) less-seen mutation called Lutino. These look like any yellow-backed Gouldian, but they have red eyes. It is said to be a mutation of the green back, but it is recessive and purportedly not sex-linked. Some sources say that some of the Lutinos exhibit feathers like those of the blue-faced parrot finch, as if they were cross-bred.[xviii] In these birds the eumalin, the substance that produces black in feathers, is miniscule or non-existent. This leaves only the yellow (lutein) in the feathers. Blue will convert to white, and the skin is paler than that of normal birds.

198   TANYA LOGAN

An offshoot of Lutino is an albino, obtained by crossing a lutino with a blue back. Remembering that the plumage is yellow in a lutino, and that the lutino in turn changes blue to white, these finches are colored white and have red eyes with pale legs and feet. A black head will be presented as pure white. Yellow heads, which are straw-colored in a blue-back, will present as beige.

9 I Don't Feel Like School Today

Illness and Treatment

Having an ill bird in the flock, or a sudden death, can be frustrating. Birds hide their illness, which means by the time we realize there is a problem it is often too late to treat it. Therefore part of bird-keeping is to observe each bird every day so that we know their habits. Additionally, stress in birds can lead quickly to disease, so minimizing stressors only makes sense. Some stress-inducing situations include

- Draft or chill
- Predators (dogs, cats, rats) in close proximity
- Transport
- Catching/handling
- Poor nutrition
- Overcrowding

Many of us reside in areas that do not have access to avian veterinarians, or they do not treat finches, or it is cost prohibitive. I will try to provide as much information as I can about illnesses, but the treatments mentioned here are anecdotal only. I am **not** a veterinarian; I have researched these illnesses through veterinary journals and books, discussions with experienced breeders, as well as plenty of personal experience. I have consulted with veterinarians who specialize in aviculture. I have treated my own birds when I felt the diagnosis was obvious but usually I defer to the vet.

I believe that **nothing** supersedes a trip to the veterinarian when your bird is ill. Please always defer to your avian vet's advice over any that you might read, including in this book! Be especially wary when using the Internet, where information could be incorrect, outdated, or important components may be left out.

I have two avian-specific veterinarians, one is my regular vet who is about 20 minutes away who examines my birds for their yearly checkups, will run lab tests for me quickly and performs necropsies (autopsies of dead birds). The other is a concierge vet who comes to my home and observes not only the sick bird(s) but also the entire aviary and environment. It is well worth paying hundreds for a concierge service when there's an unknown illness that has killed 4 or 5 birds already.

This veterinarian can see the whole picture and observe any husbandry skills that might be lacking in my aviary. He removes dropping samples from each cage, swabs crops and vents, and performs necropsies -- and gets back to me with an answer. I mention this to let the reader know there are avian veterinarians available even in small towns. Finding one *before* the birds become ill is vital.

Infections may be treated with one of a number of antibiotics, the trick being diagnosis of the disease. Whereas a veterinarian can look at slides and run tests to determine which strain has invaded the bird, we have only guesswork at our command. Using a shotgun approach by throwing every medication available at the bird is useless and can increase stress. Additionally, overuse of antibiotics can render them ineffective.

Preventive Care

You've heard the saying "an ounce of prevention is worth a pound of cure." This goes doubly so with finch care. Basic chores like removing all visible droppings (AVD) and changing the food and water every day help prevent sickness. Cleanliness, careful quarantine, and preventive medicine will go a long way in keeping illness out of the aviary. So will removing a bird to isolation and providing warmth; sometimes it will recover with no further intervention. We'll cover more preventive care further on in the chapter.

A Sick Bird

So if birds hide their sickness, what do we observe that alerts us to a problem?

Signs of illness can include:

- Sleeping a lot or other behavioral changes
- Puffed up
- Posture change on the perch (droopy)
- Sitting on the cage floor
- Weight change (you'd have to handle him or weigh him regularly to see this, or feel the keel bone to

see if it is sharp)
- Change in droppings' color or looseness, especially if they are clinging to the vent
- Increased eating or drinking, or not eating at all
- Long molt, no molt, ragged-ended feathers
- Wings carried lower than normal
- Sneezing, coughing, tail bobbing, clicking with the breath
- Discharge from the nares

When a bird appears fluffed or lethargic, catch him gently and examine him from head to toe. Part the feathers in the belly region to study the keel bone and internal organs, which can be seen through the skin. Look for signs of dehydration or malnutrition (a sharp keel bone). Study the nares for discharge. Hold him close to your ear and listen for whistling or clicking as he breathes. Look at the feet to see if they have wounds. Study the skin under the feathers to see if cysts are present.

One of the most important tools to have on hand is a small hospital cage ready to use at the first sign of illness. The bird is moved to the hospital cage and heated to 86 degrees F (30 C) through the use of a ceramic heating bulb. It is important to the rest of the flock that the sick bird is removed from them ASAP.

Provide the usual food and water; locate the perch low in the cage if necessary. The floor of the hospital cage is covered with clean papers or paper towels in order to monitor the droppings. Ideally the cage is located away from busy family activity, so the finch will not encounter added stress. If he is not eating, he can die within hours, so glucose-enriched electrolytes are kept on hand to restore energy and stimulate the appetite. These can be beak-dosed if necessary. If he's eating or drinking at all, put the electrolytes or 1/3-strength vitamins into the water source.

*This is a slow process.

A few Illnesses One Might Encounter, and How a Vet Might Treat Them

Colds, Wheezing, Respiratory Illness

Birds react strongly to damp environments and dust, including the dust that is produced during molt. The use of dehumidifiers and air purifiers can improve these situations quickly. Even opening a window, if the air outdoors is dry and warm, can help. If the room has been damp, it is worth checking all food including seed for signs of mold; if it is questionable, remove it all and start over with fresh food. Amoxycillin and Baycox are popular treatments that will often take care of sinus issues and respiratory distress.

The signs of a cold or respiratory illness include crusting beside the nares, breathing with an open beak, tail bobbing with breathing, sneezing, wheezing, and fluffing up. Birds fluff to keep body heat in, so this is instantly a sign that moving them to a warm hospital cage or at least installing a heat lamp is in order. Clicking while breathing could mean there is a respiratory illness, but it could also point to an air sac mite infestation. Swelling around the nare area or even over the eye are indications of an infection.

Respiratory infections (colds) cannot heal on their own in birds as they do in humans, because ours are viral but theirs are bacterial in nature. Left untreated, the illness can travel to other parts of the body. So an antibiotic is in order, but the ones off-the-shelf at a pet store may be the wrong treatment.

Please note if you have a respiratory or sinus infection yourself, be careful not to handle your birds without washing hands first, lest you transmit your germs to them.

Home Remedies for Respiratory Infections

The bird must be moved immediately to a hospital cage with heat. Make sure water and food are easily accessible; if he can't go up to perch, move them down. Sometimes they'll get better just by living under heat a few days.

Provide fresh water with ginger, honey, or pedialyte added. Freshen often, especially if adding honey which will speed up bacteria growth.

Some products to boost the immune system, thereby preventing or fighting off the illness, are probiotics, cayenne, and herbs like echinacea and chamomile. Neem leaf tea, steeped for an hour and served in place of water every other day, is a powerful antibacterial and antifungal.[5]

I use Neem tea myself in my aviary, and make sure it is on hand at all times. The ratio of tea leaves to water is 1:8. Steep for one hour, serving at room temperature. It is normally served in place of water but can also be used as a bath for mite treatment or skin infection.

However there are two problems to be aware of with Neem: the finches may not care for the taste--so they might need a little plain water each day to keep them from dehydrating. The other problem is that it may render them temporarily infertile. Since the effect is temporary, and since we are treating an already-ill bird anyway, I do not worry about this side effect--but it tells me not to treat small babies with Neem.

Changes in Droppings

Droppings are a great indicator of health, and not all changes indicate diarrhea. There are many variations in droppings that are simply the result of dietary adjustments. A bird that eats pellets will have rust colored droppings instead of green. One that eats a lot of vegetables will have a wetter, loose poop by comparison - but in this case it is not a medical emergency.

Most people use droppings as an indicator of health. By examining them and knowing what's "normal" for your flock can help to identify an illness early on and get help. Color, consistency, and number of droppings per day are what we are watching for.

A normal dropping consists of three parts: the feces, a green color (may be rust colored if the bird is eating pellet food), the urates, a chalky white portion, and the urine, the watery portion.

Below are a few of the changes that would be considered important enough to take the bird to the vet, but any change could signal illness. Don't hesitate to show the veterinarian your findings so your bird can get help early on.

Dropping is mostly urine - it is watery and has little feces or urates. This bird is probably not eating or it has a blockage.

Dropping contains seeds - this can indicate gizzard problems, canker, avian gastric yeast, or other disease.

Dropping contains bubbles – indication of infection.

Dropping has an odor – usually a sign of infection.

Urate color is off - normally these are white or off-white. If they are yellow or bright green, there is a serious problem. Psittacosis is one illness accompanied by neon green droppings, as is hepatitis.

Normal feces with watery or excess urates - could indicate a kidney problem. Occasionally is normal for that individual.

Fecal portion is grayish or contains excess liquid - could be an intestinal infection.

"Popcorn" Poo - you'll know this when you see it. Droppings are like pieces of popcorn, and they will be all or nearly all urates (which can be white, cream, or grayish). Often indicates disease of the pancreas,[xix] but can be due to a combination of intestinal infection, parasites, and/or protozoa. When people have asked me to look in on birds with this sort of droppings, they have always been living in filthy conditions.

Protozoa

Signs of protozoal infections include yellow-green diarrhea, undigested seed in droppings, dirty vent, and sleeping a lot. For a bird that has not been treated for protozoans in the past, Ronidazole 12% can be given at a ratio of 1 teaspoon to 2 quarts of drinking water. Treat for a full 7 days. If one bird has these signs, it is likely the rest of them are infected as well so it's best to treat all birds in close proximity to one another.

Diarrhea or 'Wet Vent' can be brought on by any number of things. Don't immediately assume it is a bacterial infection and serve up the antibiotics. Often stools can become loose due to stress, eating lots of greens or fruit, or eating salty foods. Diseases that can cause wet vent include coccidiosis, e. Coli, streptococcus, and others. Back off on the vegetables and see if that improves it. Remove recent stressors if possible.

Home Remedies to try for Diarrhea

When stools are loose, be sure the fresh food is not being left in the cage too long. Wash all food and water containers thoroughly and give them a bleach or F10 soak. Do not serve any more fresh food until the problem subsides, since a bird with diarrhea can go downhill quickly.

Try switching to bottled water. Sometimes the local water supply undergoes changes that do not affect us, but they affect our gentle creatures.

Make sure rodents are not entering the enclosure and soiling the food.

Give the bird a teaspoon of poppy seeds, or black tea.

If these things do not work, put apple cider vinegar into the water. The ratio is 15 ml to 1 liter. This is a fairly low dose.

If none of the above methods help the bird to improve, it is time to look toward other causes. Enteritis can be brought on by e. coli, salmonella, or a host of other bacteria. Even candidiasis "yeast infection" can be the culprit. It is impossible to diagnose without veterinary care.

Yeast

There are two types of yeast infections that affect finches: Candidiasis and Avian Gastric Yeast.

Candida is normal in the bird's digestive system, but its overgrowth is often caused by a dirty environment, stress, or improper nutrition, particularly the consumption of sugary foods.

Treating yeast is difficult, but fortunately preventing a flareup is easier. Removing old food in a timely manner, changing water often, and providing supplements that boost the immune system go a long way in preventing candidiasis, as will washing hands often during aviary care, and avoiding the use of antibiotics unless absolutely certain that they are needed. Using probiotics is said to reduce the incidence of yeast in a flock. They are inexpensive and can be given daily without harm.

One simple tool in the arsenal against yeast is apple cider vinegar (ACV). For this to be effective, it must be organic ACV with the mother intact; most health food stores carry Bragg's brand. The ratio of ACV to drinking water should be 15 ml/liter and can safely be added two days per week. This will usually prevent outbreaks of yeast.

Some breeders like to provide ACV one full week out of every four instead of weekly; do what works for you. A similar product to ACV is called Megamix, which is citric acid. If choosing to use Megamix, follow the directions given on the bottle.

Once the birds actually have a yeast infection, Nystatin is said to be one of the best anti-fungal medicines on the market. It works by remaining in the digestive tract and killing those live yeast organisms with which it comes into contact. It does not kill any other cells and can even be overdosed without issue. If nystatin fails, it is generally due to the fact that the strain itself is resistant.

It is said that Caprylic acid acts systemically and can be used to counter yeast, as can garlic. I have not tried these.

Yeast infections often accompany bacterial infections, so after running the course of antibiotics watch carefully for signs. Consider dosing with Megamix or apple cider vinegar, or treating with medication if the infection is serious. Yeast can also be brought on via feeding fresh corn or other sugar-containing foods like fruit.

Avian Gastric Yeast, or AGY is different from Candida, the type we normally consider "yeast." AGY is a megab-acteria infection affecting mainly smaller birds. They may regurgitate, sleep a lot, lose weight, and pass undigested food. Those that do recover may go on be carriers, shedding the organism via their droppings. Treatment that is usually given is a medicine called Amphotericin-B, although some claim apple cider vinegar has been somewhat successful. Others believe thyme tea served daily or a bit of cottage cheese with thyme and anise tea leaves in it will help.

AGY is a lengthy, horrible disease. A correct diagnosis and treatment may not guarantee a positive outcome.

Infections

Psittacosis, also called Ornithosis and/or parrot fever, is an extremely contagious disease that can be airborne and can transmit to humans. It is caused by the bacteria *chlamydia psittici.* The signs of psittacosis are respiratory distress and 'runny nose' as well as diarrhea. Effective treatment is doxycycline, 1/4 tsp to 500 ML (17 oz.) of water for up to 45 days, and the vet may also recommend supplementing that with ACV or following it with probiotics.

The bacterium is susceptible to heat and to my cleaner of choice, bleach, in a ratio of 1:100. However it is resistant to acids. The zoonotic risk is exceedingly high and people who come in contact with sick birds should wear gloves and masks. Even a brief exposure poses risk, especially to those with compromised immune systems. This disease is less common in finches and canaries than larger companion birds but because of its zoonotic (transmittable to humans) nature it bears discussion here.

E. Coli, Streptococcus, Staphylococcosis - these familiar-sounding illnesses can all affect finches. All three can be somewhat managed by keeping a clean, dry aviary. E. Coli is fairly common in nestlings, and it is easily identifiable by the pungent nest smell. You'll never forget it once you've experienced it.

Staphylococcosis "staph" infections are usually caused by the strain *S aureus* and can be diagnosed by a veterinarian. Typically they are treated with an antibiotic like erythromycin. Staph often enters the body via a wound, including those on the feet - a good reason to keep perches clean.

Streptococcus "strep" in birds cannot be diagnosed, since the bacteria are present in a normal, healthy bird. In one study, many budgies were tested and it was found that up to 40% carried the strep bacteria in the blood stream, but did not show signs of illness. Infection may occur in the respiratory system, the liver, heart, or in embryonic eggs.

Treatment for strep must be tested by the veterinarian, since many strains respond to doxycycline, some to erythromycin, and fewer to Baytril.

Coccidiosis, caused by a parasite, is a common disease. It will produce a black spot on the right side of the abdomen in hatchlings, which is the enlarged gall bladder. Black spots on both sides are common in juveniles. Mortality rates are high and diagnosis is difficult. In adult birds, intestines are quickly damaged. Coccidiosis outbreaks may be seen when conditions are damp -say you just had a week of rainy weather - or when birds are overcrowded, since the disease is spread through droppings. Symptoms include lethargy, weight loss, blood in droppings, and wet vents. There may be no symptoms if the bird is not under stress.

TREATMENT: Baycox, endocox, or other protozoal treatments. Be sure the label indicates it will treat coccidiosis. Dosage: Baycox - 6 ml per gallon in the drinking water for 2 days. Endocox (2.5% powder) - Mix 5 grams powder to one gallon clean water. Use as the only source of drinking water for seven days. Treat again as needed until symptoms subside. Be sure to disinfect the cage daily while treating birds.

PREVENTION: Coccidiosis outbreak can be *prevented* through the use of coccidiostats. A couple of brand names are Cocci-care (Morning Bird), Endocox, and Carlox (Dr. Rob Marshall). To prevent an outbreak in nestlings, one month before breeding treat the breeder pair with 9 ml of Endocox 2.5% per gallon of clean water. Ronex, a popular parasitic remedy, is not an effective treatment against coccidia.

Canker

Canker is caused by a protozoan, *Trichomonas*. There is more than one mutation of that protozoan, so it is possible to see different kinds of infection. We may see vomiting or frothing at the beak, followed by thinness. We might see yellow droppings or seed in the droppings. We could also see yellow lesions inside the mouth. By the time we see those, the infection is in the throat area as well and is slowly starving the bird.

TREATMENT AND PREVENTION: Canker is said to come in via a carrier bird. It is found in the mouth, trachea, crop, pharynx, and liver. It can move through the aviary via contact, droppings, bedding, and from a parent feeding a baby. A veterinarian can perform crop washes to find a carrier; but to remove canker entirely from the breeding program, the entire flock including babies should be dosed Ronidasole. Dosage should be strong, up to 4 times the normal amount for 7 days. Many people treat the aviary every 3 months since Gouldian finches are so susceptible to canker.

It is important to thoroughly disinfect the cage or aviary daily while treatment is going on. Give the weaker birds soft or liquid foods.

Scaly Legs or Scaly Face

These conditions are usually caused by mites. By the time the owner observes the scaliness, the bird has had the illness for quite some time. The bird will seem itchy and its scratching may cause lesions, which lead to secondary infection. He may have crusty spots at the corners of the beak. The mites themselves are invisible to the naked eye, but are easily seen under the microscope by a veterinarian.

These mites can be treated with Ivermectin, Moxidectin, S76 or SCATT. The treatment can be as long as 8 weeks, depending on the level of infestation. Do not pull the scales off, as this will cause bleeding.

There are also some tried-and-true home remedies. A damp Chamomile tea bag held over the affected area will help heal and loosen the scales. Grapefruit Seed extract has some anti-parasitic properties. I do not have experience in using it as a scaly face mite treatment; however others have used it under veterinarian supervision, placing up to 5 drops in one tablespoon of distilled water. Dab the infected areas with this mixture. Do not ever put full strength GSE on your bird.

One oft-repeated "remedy" that does *not* work is coating the skin with Vaseline or oil. People claim it smothers the mites. Not only is this untrue, by coating the skin bacteria is kept against the skin, making it likely to become infected.

Feather Loss

Sometimes a bird has been plucked and the owner will ask for a 'diagnosis.' The plucked bird is easy to spot because his head or neck is the only area missing plumage. Separating him from the offending party is necessary for his health.

I recently had a Gouldian finch with the most horrible, painful-looking pinfeathers across his chest. I gave him baths and dosed him with a feather-growing supplement, but he decided to pull out every single feather. It was sad and must have been painful, plus he had to go through the pain of re-growing them. It is evident in this case that the hen did not do the plucking, since it was across his chest. That was the first Gouldian I've had that self-mutilated.

Baldness in Gouldians is common. There are several factors that can lead to baldness. An easy one to cure is the presence of mites, which should have been taken care of during the initial quarantine protocol. If there is reason to believe the bird has mites but the feathers do not grow after treatment, rub betadine or chlorhexidine wash (diluted of course) directly on the head. This will usually kill off the infection that's preventing the feathers from growing.

Lack of iodine in the diet is said to lead to baldness. Gouldians are one of few birds that have a need for extra iodine. It can be provided easily via liquid drops in the drinking water or by offering kelp granules or powder in the supplement tray.

Most often the cause of baldness is a lack of vitamins. Finches that do not have access to sunlight are frequently lacking in vitamin D3. Other suspects might be iodine, B12, vitamin A, and calcium. Using quality supplements and feeding plenty of fresh foods on a regular schedule will usually have them back in full feather by the next molt.

As a last resort, I will take a bald finch outdoors for about 30 minutes every day for a week. The only two times I've had bald Gouldians, both of which arrived from other breeders as adults, this worked in bringing on feather regrowth. My hypothesis is that most birds are lacking in D3, so exposing them to sunlight helps to synthesize this and in turn other vitamins, stimulating feather growth.

There is one more reason for baldness in Gouldians, recently unearthed by a research scientist. Dr. Sarah Pryke has discovered that baldness can be brought on by stress but it also is hereditary. So if none of the above suggestions work, assume your finch has this recessive gene - and don't breed it![xx]

Injuries and Wounds

Bleeding

Wounds can come from nails being clipped too short (called "quicking"), becoming entangled in cage decor, and nips from other birds. The presence of fresh blood should always be considered a dire emergency; tiny finches can bleed out in a few moments' time.

When blood is noticed, catch the finch, rinse the wound, and use styptic powder to stop the bleeding. If styptic powder is not on hand, pack clean flour against the wound until bleeding stops. Observe the bird closely for the next 24 hours. Generally if the bleeding has stopped they're in the safe zone. It is a good precaution to separate an injured finch from the flock, move them to the hospital cage and apply heat with appropriate electrolytes and vitamins. If the bird is moving well, no longer bleeding, and seems normal it may be more stressful to remove him from the flock than to leave him.

It is worth noting that, although I have only ever rinsed wounds with water with no ill effects, many swear by the use of colloidal silver for washing them. Topical antibiotics like terramycin are recommended and are safe.

Blood Feathers

When any bird molts, the new pin feathers that emerge have a blood supply. This goes away as the feather matures, but while there is still blood inside the feather shaft, if it gets damaged it will bleed – sometimes profusely.

In order to stop the bleeding, the feather has to be removed by pulling it from the follicle. This can be done with fingers, but it's a little easier to use tweezers. Pull gently but firmly in the direction the feather was growing.

If the area still bleeds, apply flour or styptic powder and use pressure but most times it will stop without assistance. Be vigilant, as finches can bleed out from a blood feather injury.

Parasites

The majority of parasites can be prevented by the use of an ongoing protocol guarding against them, including treating and quarantining new birds that are brought into the aviary. Some, though, are particularly persistent and it is possible to find an infestation even in the best of aviaries.

Air Sac Mites are a good example of this. They are common in Gouldians, so much so that one veterinarian stated that they were present in nearly every case he examined. These are tiny mites that invade the respiratory system, primarily residing in the air sacs, located in the lungs.

Birds infested with air sac mites may not show any symptoms at all, or they may show breathing problems like clicking, whistling, or tail-bobbing as they breathe. They also might appear to salivate.

Because air sac mites can live in the lungs without symptoms, yet can cause severe and even fatal infection during times of stress, it is necessary to administer medication as a preventive and sometimes again as a treatment if needed. It is possible for these mites to transfer from one bird to another via perches, nesting material, and even food. Therefore cages and nests must be disinfected at the same time the birds are treated.

Mites live an average of 6 days, and the incubation period is 3 weeks so the treatment must take that into consideration. S76, Ivermectin products and SCATT (moxidectin) are the medications of choice. In the U.S., I know people who are now treating with S76 and SCATT at the same time to try to rid their aviary of ASM.

The dosage is as follows: S76 in the water 2 days each week for at least 3 weeks. The mixing ratio according to the manufacturer is 5 ml to 2 quarts of water. Mix fresh daily, and clean the cage, nest, and the area around the cage thoroughly with Avian Insect Liquidator or another miticide.

When using SCATT, place one drop onto the skin (not the feathers) behind the head, on the thigh, or under the wing. Repeat 21 days later. Do not use more often than 21 days apart; this medication goes into the bloodstream and remains effective for 3 weeks, so in this case more is not better.

Blood Mites are microscopic and can feed on humans, unlike feather mites. They and their eggs can remain dormant for months, which makes them terribly difficult to eradicate.

Feather Mites are common and will cause feathers to have a rough appearance as well as causing lethargy, anemia, and respiratory infections.

Burrowing Mites (*epidermoptic* mites) get under the skin, causing it to have a bumpy, almost crusty appearance. These are especially interesting to us as Gouldian owners because when other causes have been ruled out, ***burrowing mites could be causing baldness.*** Burrowing mites can be treated as other mites (described below) with some success but they are more likely than other types to lead to secondary infection. This is due to the finch digging or scratching at the skin.

Sticktight Fleas or *echidnophaga gallonacea* can be a problem in tropical or sub-tropical climates. The fleas gather around the head area, especially the eyes. They can be treated with Avian Insect Liquidator sprayed directly on the bird per package instructions.

Treating for Mites

In order to treat for mites, both the environment and the birds have to be treated. If one bird is found to have any type of mite, all the others in the vicinity must be treated in order to prevent reinfestation. Additionally, all nests, cages, and the entire room should be treated. Here's how.

You will need SCATT, S76, Avian Insect Liquidator (AIL), and Diatomaceous Earth (DE).

Treat the bird externally with SCATT on the thigh or back of neck. As an extra dose, treat internally by dosing S76 in the water. At the same time, clean the cages and entire room thoroughly, then spray the cage, tray below, nest box, and surrounding area with AIL. After this has dried, sprinkle DE around the baseboards if no pets can reach it, and in the drop tray below the cage. Place some in the bottom of the nest box. Continue to treat the room with DE for at least a month or more (remember, these mites have life cycles and hatch rates - we've got to get rid of the new ones hatching out). Re-apply the SCATT in 21 days. Evaluate after the first month to determine whether the mites are gone. If so, the bird should seem less agitated or itchy, feathers lost should be regrowing, and so on. If not, continue treating for as many months as it takes; scaly face or scaly legs may require up to 8 weeks of consistent treatment.

**Note: If after a couple of months it seems that the products aren't working, it is time to evaluate the *environment* again. The treatment area may need to expand to include window sills, drop ceilings, closets, or even other pets.

Symptoms and What They May Mean

Since diagnosing illness is seemingly impossible, I've tried to present characteristics of each ailment to provide the reader with a best guess to determine what ails their flock.

Watery droppings, especially after a few days of rain or high humidity – coccidiosis

Smelly wet nest or large number of nestling deaths- e.coli

Large yellow mass in the throat or crop, bird adjusting crop often - canker

Yellow/green diarrhea accompanied by dirty feathers, constant sleep: protozoal infection.

Baldness: can be mite-induced, lack of vitamins, stress, hereditary, or less often, bacterial skin infection.

Failure to breed: Poor libido can be brought on by an infection, like coccidiosis or canker in the aviary. It can be due to stress. It can also be due to lack of nutrients.

Providing supplemental vitamins and micronutrients, probiotics, and checking the nutritional value of the foods given may change this condition.

Hens that do not breed may be ill or simply not in breeding condition. There have been numerous times that I believed a pair 'should' be ready, only to find they went into molt the next week! Please see the breeding chapter for more information.

Stress

I believe that finches can often be under tremendous stress without the owner(s) being aware of it. Sometimes predators like dogs or cats are present. Even larger parrots can cause stress in the finch flock. If the flock is moving away to the farthest, highest corner -- they are feeling predator stress even if the owner does not believe they are threatened. Birds cannot reason that the cage bars will keep them safe; instinct tells them to get away but they cannot because of their cage or aviary boundaries. This is the time to remove the dog or cat, or add gates, fencing, or other boundaries to keep them out.

Occasionally a cage is located in a busy area (a business lobby, for example) or in a part of the room where people are able to move around all sides. This is an extreme stress situation for the birds. If it is not possible to relocate the cage against a wall, the back of the cage, or back and 2 sides can be covered with cardboard, posterboard, or fabric. This gives the birds a sense of safety.

Extreme temperatures or temperatures fluctuating more than 10 degrees F can trigger stress-related illness. Ten degrees doesn't seem like much to us, which is why I mention it.

Poor nutrition, like vitamin deficiency or even lack of certain amino acids will lead to several issues. Although some signs are evident, like balding or poor feather quality, others are not obvious at all. The solution is to give the broadest availability of high-quality foods at all times. Supplements may or may not be advisable, depending on whether pellet foods are fortified and how much fresh food is part of the diet; a veterinarian will advise best in this situation.

Molt

One of the most difficult times for a finch is during molt. It is extremely hard on the body, which has to replace every single feather. Molt can last months depending on the bird's condition. An owner may see E. coli, ornithosis, yeast infections, or parasites during this period. Provide nutritional support and watch carefully when birds are in molt. Some extra sleeping during this time is normal but constant sleeping through the day is an indication of illness.

Amino acids are not generally supplied completely in the diet, and the lack of them at molting time can lead to slow molt or even death from stress. There are products on the market containing amino acids and minerals to encourage feather growth. I strongly recommend them.

Note: Do not give the feather enhancing supplements to birds that don't need them; sometimes this drives them into molt.

Overcrowding is a common cause of stress. New owners especially do not realize the amount of space these little finches really require, and if they are allowed to breed, cages or aviaries can fill up past capacity in only one good breeding season. A crowded cage full of stressed, bickering

THE GOULDIAN FINCH HANDBOOK   221

birds is a fertile ground for illness to take hold. Better to separate them out before this becomes a problem.

To resolve the overcrowding problem, obviously more cages -- or fewer birds! - are in order. But the stress can be eased somewhat by placing more fake or real plants in the cage, or by the addition of stress perches. These are perches with a 'roof' and dividers so that several finches can perch at once, but they have their own space, and the next finch over can't see them. For an overcrowded cage that will be rectified soon, these may be a good temporary solution.

Egg binding (see egg problems in the breeding chapter)

Thirst

Thirsty finches will often squint, or "squinch" their eyes (hold them closed but in a squeezed-tight way). I finally figured this out on my own, after spending about 2 weeks asking veterinarians and breeders why my blue-backed male Gouldian was squinting. They all stared at me and shrugged, doubtless wondering whether to call the men in white coats. That bird died; he was dehydrated.

If a bird that is suddenly squinting and does not have an eye injury, try administering water and electrolytes It is worthwhile to also check its water source, change the water, and begin observing its behavior. If still squinting after 24 hours move it to a hospital cage and give NV powder or other vitamins and clean fresh water. After the initial dose or two of electrolytes, water with diluted vinegar may also be given.

Twirling

A twirling bird will suddenly seem to have "lost their balance. They twist their head, fall, and seem disoriented. There are many theories about twirling. Some say it is a lack of vitamins or minerals, a head injury, an ear infection, or a genetic problem. People have claimed to successfully treat twirling syndrome with Nystatin or Medistatin, Trimethoprim Sulfa, and/or trace minerals, although *Avian Medicine* states "antibiotic therapy does not change the course of the disease."[xxi] I have never had a twirler; if I had one I would not breed it.

Dehydration can occur on very hot days, at times that the air conditioner has gone on the blitz, or as a result of mistakes (forgetting to provide fresh water). Sometimes the ball in the water bottle sticks and goes unnoticed. As soon as one realizes the bird is suffering, provide fresh clean water, down low if necessary, fortified with a product like Thrive, Quik Gel, Vitalize, or even pedialyte from the grocery store. I give my thirsty guys a shallow bath also, figuring that it can only help to have water on the skin and feathers too. Finches can become critically ill within 24 hours of not having water and many die sooner than that.

Weight Loss

Losing weight in spite of eating may have one of several causes. Birds that have lost considerable weight are referred to as "going light" which is a descriptive term and not a diagnosis. A few breeders use the term in place of a specific illness, Avian Gastric Yeast (AGY) but it's an incorrect terminology. Candidiasis, AGY, enteritis, and many other illnesses involve weight loss as a symptom.

Weight loss in a Gouldian, even a large amount, is difficult to see. Usually it is noticed when you catch a finch for nail trims or to move cages. That's when you feel the sharp keel bone and realize there is a problem. Weight loss of this magnitude cannot be ignored, and the underlying illness must be addressed before trying to put weight back on the sick finch.

How to Treat an Entire Aviary

When illness arrives, remove the sick bird or birds to a hospital cage as quickly as possible. With Gouldians, sometimes you are suddenly dealing with several sick or dying birds. To safeguard the flock, more steps must be taken.

First, study the aviary and see what could be causing the illness. Are there food scraps caught along the edges of the cage? Is there a buildup of droppings on a perch, grate, or other location?

- ○ Scrub down the offending areas and remove all substrates. Disinfect cages with F10.
- ○ Scrub and disinfect feeders and drinkers. Make sure to change drinking water once daily.
- ○ If moldy or moth-ridden food is suspected, take away those foods and buy new ones.
- ○ Do not feed soft food or sprouts during this time.
  - • If not using ACV on a regular basis, add it to the drinking water now, along with vitamins and other supplements (not in the water at the same time as ACV). Add calcium to the water or offer ground eggshells.
- ○ Review all protocols to be sure health, cleanliness, and sanitizing are covered.

224 TANYA LOGAN

Write your avian vet's number here--before you need it:

Name: Number:

After hours call:

ASPCA National Animal Poison Control Center (24 hr) 888-426-4435

From The Gouldian Finch Handbook ~~ Tanya Logan You may share this document in its entirety. Please do not alter it in any way.

Finch First Aid Kit

Must have items for
  Finch First Aid:

Name	Use:
Styptic powder or stick	stop bleeding
Hydrogen Peroxide	Clean wounds
Neosporin	treat minor cuts and scratches
Syringe	administering medicine or food/water
Eye dropper	administering liquids or medication

Pedialyte, Quikgel, ER Formula, NV Powder, or Thrive	for dehydrated birds or birds not eating
Leg band cutters	emergency removal of leg bands (or have veterinarian do it)
Mineral oil or cooking oil	rub on vent of egg bound hens
Liquid calcium	emergency treatment of eggbound hens
S76 or SCATT	routine treatment for mites
Probiotic	improve digestion after illness or antibiotic use
Ronex	Treats protozoan infections
Worm Away	Wormer
Colloidal silver	treats crusty eyes and wounds
Liquid Oxygen, vitamin C	removes heavy metals/detoxes body (for poison ingestion)
Amoxitex	Bacterial antibiotic
Cocci-care or Medpet 4-in-1	coccidiosis; medpet also treats paratyphoid, canker, e. coli

Trimethoprim Sulfa	treats e. coli, paratyphoid, coccidian, salmonella. Safe for nesting birds and their babies.
Doxyvet or doxycycline	bacterial/ chlamydial anitbiotic, for respiratory, sinus infection
Medstatin	Candida (yeast infection)
Erythromycin	Campylobacter and other

Disinfectant/viricide, such as Virkon S, KD cleanser, F-10, or Pet Focus.

Hospital cage: Small cage or glass tank, heat source, food and water sources. Shallow dishes are best for the hospital cage.

Preventive Care

Routines, medications, supplements

I would much rather perform preventative care than attempt to treat a bird once it falls ill -- wouldn't you? So I provide my birds with the best routines and supplemental products that I can in hopes that they will reduce or eliminate potential illnesses.

Routines

Birds, like other pets, thrive on routine. They expect to be fed and watered at the same time daily; they enjoy the clock-like (or sun-like) lights on/lights out routine. Therefore, we should attempt to feed, water, and light the room on a schedule. One system is to feed and water about 12 hours apart (when the daylight is 14 hours long) and 10 hours apart when it's 'winter' with 12-hour daylight shifts. I keep all lights on timers, and they are staggered a few minutes apart to simulate sunrise and sunset.

In addition to lighting, feeding can be set to match up with Gouldians' natural patterns. There tends to be a flurry of activity, including eating, first thing in the morning and again about an hour before lights out. So those are good times to feed.

I do this by offering fresh sprouts and chop about 9 a.m. At this time I also check or change the drinkers. In the evening, I change papers and water, and put in a dry mix from C4AW.org. Here's my video about that: https://youtu.be/WaaOEFb54c8

Beak and Nail Trims

It is sometimes possible to avoid trimming beaks and nails by using natural branches or cement perches, but usually nails need a trim every couple of months. It is easy to trim them using a (human) baby nail clipper or a special bird nail clipper. They can also be filed using an emery board.

Beaks are a little more difficult and a bit dangerous, as trimming too close can cause bleeding and can cut into the many nerves located in the beak. The goal in trimming the beak is to get the top and bottom beaks meeting evenly.

Overgrown beaks should always be handled by a veterinarian. For those who may not have access to an avian vet, beaks can be managed by using small nail clippers and clipping a tiny bit of the beak off, or by filing each side gently with dental files. The file is safer for beginners. File only in one direction, from back to front, checking progress often. Usually one treatment is enough, but sometimes a second is necessary about a month later.

Causes for Long Beaks in Young (Juvenile) Gouldians

If more than one beak in the aviary becomes overgrown, it is worth investigating the underlying cause. There can be many causes for elongated beaks. In general, a long beak could be a sign of physical damage, where the beak has been injured by hitting the wire on the cage, or even by being caught in the wire or inside the nest. The body attempts to repair itself by growing new tissue, and the injury could result in abnormal growth.

Many times the beak grows too long because the bird either doesn't have access to a roughened perch where he can wipe his beak, or he simply doesn't wipe it well. If he has a cement or sand perch available, it's worth a try to move it near the drinker where he "has" to use it.

Probably the most common cause of long, overgrown beaks in young Gouldians is vitamin related. The usual culprit in the case of deficiency is Vitamin A, especially if the birds in question are on a seed-only or seed-mostly diet. I find that if I overfeed with protein foods, my young in certain families will have elongated beaks, so I suspect that too much protein could be a culprit. I can usually

THE GOULDIAN FINCH HANDBOOK 229

file down the beak and back off on the protein, and the problem resolves.

Scaly face mites are often first recognized when the beak tissue overgrows. These parasites, properly called *knemidokptes* mites, burrow into the beak tissue and cause overgrowth. Avoid them by treating periodically with SCATT.

Polyomavirus can cause longer beaks, as well as nestling and fledgling deaths and poor feathers. If these have taken place, the survivors are often carriers of the disease. They may have elongated beaks and feather damage. If you feel your bird(s) may be suffering from polyomavirus, one deceased bird can be sent for histopathology; if the outbreak is severe enough, some bird owners will even sacrifice a bird to get the full scientific study performed and get a definitive answer.

Another way to rid the flock of polyomavirus is to close the aviary and stop breeding for at least two years. If no new birds are introduced, and no young birds are present, the virus will die off.

Of course, it's always possible that genetics plays a role in elongated beaks. If they happen consistently in one family, it's worth further investigation.

Supplements

Every single day, a bird needs at least 40 essential nutrients. Furthermore, they do not store nutrients -- and food passes through their system in under 2 hours.

Please know that it is extremely easy to over-supplement finches, what with the myriad of products available on the market. The last thing a reader should do is serve daily pellets AND vitamins AND supplements that contain vitamins AND fresh foods (you guessed it, more vitamins).

230   TANYA LOGAN

This would result in an overdose of one or many vitamins, resulting in illness or death. I hope that every reader will err on the side of caution where this is concerned.

However, birds do need some supplementation, and one can observe signs that might indicate various needs. For example, a bird lacking in Vitamin B12 or D3 will often exhibit head baldness. (This can also be due to other causes.) Hens laying shell-less eggs need more calcium; so do those that are fluffy but otherwise do not seem ill. And studies show that more than half of pet birds are deficient in Vitamin A.

There is no one-size-fits-all solution for finches, both because very few (credible) nutrition studies have been conducted on them, and because every aviary set-up differs, as do food sources. Small birds' diets are often merely a scaled-down suggestion of larger bird diets, which may not meet their needs adequately.

Let's begin with calcium and its counterparts, D3 and phosphorus. we know that by ensuring the right levels of calcium we will have:

- Healthier hens
- Larger clutches
- Better hatch rates
- More live chicks

So how much calcium do they need?

Technically, a non-breeding, non-growing Gouldian finch needs 0.5% calcium daily in its diet. However, that number can vary considerably for various situations (say, a hen laying eggs). Calcium is necessary for bone formation, egg formation, and balancing the phosphorus and vitamin D3 ratio.[xxii]

Most people supplement with a cuttlefish bone and assume that is enough calcium for their birds. The problem with this is that cuttlebone is difficult to absorb into the bloodstream. And breeding hens need more calcium anyway; they use up calcium very quickly. Imagine this: Most hens only contain enough calcium in their bones to lay three eggs. So they lay the three, and they're depleted and unhealthy. Any further eggs that are laid will be sub-par: misshapen or shell-less. Neither of these is a condition you want your hen in, right?

The simplest way to provide calcium is by supplementing it in the drinking water two to three times per week. Foods that contain calcium include spinach, turnip greens, almonds, flax seeds, and kale.

Can we overdose calcium?

Yes. Calcium levels that are too high can cause kidney stones, constipation, pain, and sometimes prevents chicks from being able to hatch (because the shell is to thick). Too much calcium may also prevent the ability to absorb other nutrients, such as iron.

Protein

Like humans, birds need protein for energy as well as growing feathers, repairing muscle, and hormone production. Providing protein is quite easy, assuming we feed more than a seed-only diet. Pellets are fairly low in protein—a popular brand, Roudybush, only contains 11% protein. Adult Gouldians need 12% and growing or breeding birds may need protein levels of up to 20 percent. Fortunately, birds love egg and other protein-laden foods.

The easiest way to provide protein is by adding either hardboiled egg or a supplemental food to the diet, like Breeder's Blend or Miracle Meal. Breeder's Blend is sprinkled on the soft food; Miracle Meal is a food that can be offered free choice. Another great option is hemp seed. I have recently found bags of ground hemp seed at the grocery, which can be sprinkled over their fresh food each day.

One or two hard boiled eggs mixed with a can of plain breadcrumbs will be readily eaten and contains a good ratio of carbohydrates to protein. Mealworms, either live or freeze-dried, are another great source of protein.

Carbohydrates

People tend to think carbohydrates are bad, probably equating them with human diets and our propensity to label carbs as such. But carbohydrates provide fuel, and may be the only way the nervous system can repair itself. Carbohydrates are available to our birds through the use of seeds, vegetables, and fruit.

Robert Black, in his article "Carbohydrates: The Good and Bad Points" suggests that we tend to overdo carbohydrates for birds. Black recommends fewer carbohydrates and more protein and fats in birds' diets.[xxiii]

Some Nutritional Supplements

Activated Charcoal – used to enhance digestion. Helps flush toxins from the body. The birds instinctively eat it when they don't feel well. Can add to grit mix or serve separately. It is said to prevents sour stomach/sour crop by lessening acid. Charcoal blocks the uptake of A, B2, and K so only given in small amounts.

THE GOULDIAN FINCH HANDBOOK   233

Alfalfa - provides antioxidants and amino acids. Use the powder form.

Aloe - moves a slow crop and soothes inflamed tissues from yeast. The recommended brand names are Aloe Detox or Herbal Aloe Force.

Bee Pollen - is chock full of vitamins and amino acids. It may also help strengthen the immune system.

Cattle Mineral Powder – easily accepted supplement with many trace elements.

Cayenne Pepper Powder –Applied topically, it can staunch the flow of blood from a wound or cut.

Charcoal – deactivates toxins in the gut. Birds may prefer powdered over granules.

Cinnamon – fights against infection and respiratory distress. Powdered cinnamon can be added to the soft food mix.

Clay – deactivates toxins through binding.

Cuttlefish bone – Provides a small amount of calcium, helps keep beaks trimmed.

Diatomaceous Earth – purchase food grade, not the swimming pool filter type. It kills on contact, which means it will not kill organisms it can't get to (like air sac mites in the lungs). DE does cut back on the parasitic load, if the bird has any.

Egg shell – best calcium source. If boiled, serve as is; if raw, rinse and microwave 2 to 3 minutes.

E-powder - full of B vitamins and amino acids, e-powder was created with breeding in mind. Use it as a supplement for chicks and tired Gouldian parents for instant energy.

Elderberries – a favorite food, it boosts the immune system. They are sold dried and need to be ground.

Epsom Salt – a little dissolved in drinking water is said to assist with intestinal tract blockage and reduce diarrhea.

F-vite is a calcium, vitamin, and mineral powder that birds enjoy. It replaces grit, cuttle bone and salt blocks.

Garlic Juice –Commercially prepared, or made by steeping minced garlic in water then straining out the solids. Added to the drinking water, it will help boost immune systems and increase respiratory health. Garlic is also a natural wormer and mite repellent.

Grape Seed Extract (GSE) can be used in place of ACV as it is both anti-fungal and anti-parasitic.

Gentian Violet, which can be purchased at the pharmacy, is useful when yeast patches are showing in the mouth. Apply to the mouth and crop with a q-tip/ cotton bud. The tissue that is infected with yeast will then look purple. Treat daily for 3 days; lesions should begin to disappear. Sometimes yeast will cause the crop to continually "inflate;" gentian violet should help calm this.

Hearty Bird - by Morning Bird. It's a complete vitamin/ mineral supplement, except it contains no iodine. Because iodine is important for Gouldians, it should be supplemented separately if using Hearty Bird or similar.

Herb Salad - Many breeders say that Herb Salad (TM) should be provided at all times. Finches can select the parts of the salad that address their vitamin deficiencies or health issues before they become evident to the owner. This early prevention can help lessen the mortality rate, especially with small chicks. Herb salad also helps strengthen the immune system in stressed or recently ill birds.

Honey – A natural antiseptic that is said to keep wounds free from infection.

Iodine, either as a liquid supplement or by feeding kelp prevents balding in many cases and is said to improve infertility. A lack of iodine can lead to wheezing and clicking while breathing, which is often erroneously attributed to air sac mites. If the birds have already been treated for

ASM, look toward iodine deficiency or illness. I have seen many people re-treat unnecessarily for ASM when it had already been done.

Kelp powder - supplies the iodine needed, as well as potassium, calcium, magnesium and iron. Sprinkle it on the soft food. Many people say their birds will not eat the powdered kelp supplement so try sprinkling it on boiled eggs or mixing with other favorite foods.

Linoleic acid, an omega 3 fatty acid, comes primarily from nuts, seeds, and vegetable oils.[xxiv] It is used to create hormones and is a natural anti-inflammatory.[xxv]

Liquid Calcium - can help an egg-bound hen pass the egg. A few drops direct to the beak every hour or two for small birds every hour until egg is passed.

Molasses – Use sparingly to avoid diarrhea. Contains an abundance of nutrients and minerals beneficial to a bird recovering from illness or stress. Also helps flush toxins in case of poisoning or botulism.

Neem tea – used to treat for mites and lice, bacteria, and fungal infections. Boil a handful of tea leaves, steep for an hour, strain, and offer as a bath and/or as the sole drinking water. Watch for signs of dehydration in case they refuse to drink it.

Probiotics help with digestion; they are especially important after a round of antibiotics. They may help with other issues like yeast prevention and hormone regulation, and strengthen gut flora. They are safe to use daily.

Prebiotics differ from probiotics in that prebiotics don't contain the bacteria; instead, they promote the growth of good bacteria. Probiotics are the 'good' bacteria, that help balance the gut flora.

Pumpkin seed (ground) is eaten readily and works against tapeworm and roundworm.

Saline Solution – can be used to clean eyes, nares, and wounds.

Spirulina - a protein and calcium supplement.

Tea Bags – Cold tea (black or green, decaf only) said to treat diarrhea. Use as the sole source as drinking water for several days.

Thyme along with garlic helps rid them of ascarids and the hookworms.

Wormwood (*artemisia annua*) is used against parasites and bacteria in the intestinal tract.

Vinegar

Treatment with raw apple cider vinegar is a solution (but not a cure) to yeast infestations, both in hand-feeding chicks and adults suffering from Candida. Signs of Candida include very sudden illness or very sudden fluffing up. This can be caused by extremely wet or humid weather. Candida also accompanies a myriad of other diseases, so treating for it while not treating for the underlying illness will not have the best results.

ACV is sort of a probiotic, although you will hear it incorrectly referred to as an antibiotic. My veterinarian recommends 15 ml per Liter.

Also for crop problems use ACV at a solution of 2 T to gallon. Use it one week out of every quarter as a preventive or two days per week. It is said to stimulate the immune system also.

If yeast infection is apparent on the skin, apply diluted raw ACV daily.

Note that heating vinegar causes it to emit dangerous toxic fumes. Birds can die if subjected to vinegar being used in a dishwasher or coffee maker.

Quarantine - How and Why

Quarantine is simply removing a sick or injured finch from the vicinity of all other birds, and perhaps all other pets, in the household. This is done both to protect the one you are quarantining and the others in the aviary, flight, or family. Quarantine is necessary any time there is an illness or suspected illness. It can also be useful when a finch has been pecked or otherwise harassed, to prevent further harm. **Quarantine is mandatory when a finch is new to the aviary.** By using good protocols in your aviary, you will ensure that the new finch does not pass on disease or parasites to the others.

Please take this seriously and do not learn the hard way; there are many stories of owners losing 2, 10, and 200 finches due to lack of quarantine or incorrect isolation procedures. Of course we are all eager to move new birds into the aviary, but it is not worth the risk of losing some or even all the birds. There is a worksheet on the next page for the reader to use for completion of a custom quarantine plan. Creating and using the protocol will go a very long way in preventing problems in the aviary.

Quarantine will generally invoke the use of a hospital cage and, if you are quarantining due to illness, a heat source. For new stock, a regular cage will suffice. It is best for the quarantine area not to share air, including heating/cooling systems, with the regular aviary but it is not always possible to separate them to this extent; so we do the best we can.

A hospital cage is the term used for a separate "home" for a sick or ailing finch. Moving it away from others can protect it from further injury and/ or prevent the spread of disease to the rest of the flock. The hospital cage can be as simple as a 2- to 10-gallon glass fish tank with a heating pad underneath. It could also be a small bird

238 TANYA LOGAN

cage with a heater or heat lamp The cage is small to give us ease of catching the finch and to prevent him from wasting energy flying.

Diagnosing Illness

For birds that have been quarantined due to illness, utilize the quarantine period as an opportunity to deeply observe the bird's behavior and health. If you aren't sure what is going on, sometimes the heat and separation are enough to allow self-healing to take place.

I'll give the usual caveat, it is always best to take a finch to your certified avian veterinarian in order to find out what is wrong with him. I realize that many people live in areas where that is impossible. For those, a bit of self-diagnosis is required. It is best to learn all one can in order to recognize the signs and symptoms of the most common illnesses. That way there will be at least an educated guess when determining which medications to use.

When to quarantine

A finch that has shown fluffed feathers, lethargy, wet vent or little to no appetite should be immediately quarantined and given heat. It may be warm inside a home, but fluffing indicates an attempt to self-heat, so a temperature of 85- or 86-degrees F is preferred. This can be a heating pad or reptile warmer on the bottom of the cage, a light or a ceramic heat bulb near the top of the cage. A newer product consists of vertical heated panels mounted at the side of the cage. No matter which type is used, it must be entirely safe; the bird should not be able to touch a hot bulb or overheated cage parts. Take care that it does not overheat, especially if it is covered at night.

If you find a finch on the bottom of the cage for an extended period of time, consider this an emergency and move it to quarantine right away.

Finches that have been pecked excessively, have an injury, or have bled after nail clipping may also be quarantined. Basically *any time a bird seems "off"* removing it to quarantine would be the most responsible move.

A hen that has passed an egg (especially if it's a soft-shelled egg) and remains on the bottom of the cage needs to be put into quarantine right away. If she has passed a normal egg but seems off, she should probably visit the quarantine area for a while. Do not worry about the egg, as they do not begin incubating eggs right away. If needed, place the egg under another hen. However it is possible that the male will take care of the nest while the hen is away. I recently had a hen I thought was egg bound (she wasn't) that I moved to the quarantine cage for two days. The male seemed absent from the aviary; I found him caring for the nest. He was happy to turn duties back over to his mate when she returned to the cage.

When isolating a bird, provide the regular food and water that he is used to on the normal schedule. I try to use the same style of food containers and drinkers as well. If the finch is resting on the bottom, provide good footing; newspaper will work fine in both glass tanks and cages with grates.

It is often advisable to line the cage or tank with paper towels or plain white paper during the quarantine period so that the droppings can be observed and described if necessary. Color, amount of wetness, and comparison to the bird's normal droppings are all a part of the diagnosis. As a finch owner, you will become used to discussing poop color, runniness, etc. Droppings are the easiest way to observe what is going on with a bird. There is more information about dropping changes at the beginning of this chapter.

For an exhaustively complete discussion of droppings and their meanings, I have a video on You Tube that I call the Poop talk. (Its real name is Gouldian Finch Health and I am **not** a poopologist). Here's a link: https://youtu.be/1PeuOKSEOTU

Nests are unnecessary in the hospital cage. Perches can be used; place them low if the finch is weak or injured.

Treatment During Quarantine

If the appetite is waning, there are electrolyte products that can be used: Guardian Angel, Energize, and Vitalize to name a few. They work much like Pedialyte or Gatorade do for humans, providing energy and vitamins. In fact, if you do not have access to the bird-related brands, it is possible to dilute Pedialyte (found in the same aisle as Gatorade at the pharmacy, or near human baby food at the grocery) with at least 50% water. Provide seed or pellets as usual of course, and water at all times. Since the bird is feeling weak, make sure the food and water are accessible and not harder to reach than usual.

How long to quarantine?

With illness, the quarantine should last until the antibiotics are finished, or until the bird seems better "plus" about two days. If follow-up care is a must, it may be easier to keep him in the hospital area a little longer. Example: you've finished a round of antibiotics and want to administer a round of probiotics *to this bird only*. Keeping him in the hospital cage makes sense.

Another example: you felt that the bird had yeast, and you've treated with gentian violet. His droppings have not returned to normal. In this case, the yeast (candidiasis) may still be present; the bird is better off staying in the hospital cage for further observation.

For new arrivals, a minimum of 30 days is necessary. You will find that veterinarians differ in their expectations of quarantine, and some recommend 45 or even 90 days' time. This allows them to show symptoms for any illness that was brewing or masked upon arrival. Go ahead and treat them with the good health regimen, and provide food, water, and vitamins/supplements in the usual manner.

I will admit that I occasionally do not quarantine over 30 days, but that is only when I am being stupid. No, that was a joke. It is only when I have purchased a finch from someone I know extremely well who follows similar strict guidelines as I do; that way I know feel fairly certain that the incoming finch will not transmit disease or parasites to my flock. I still quarantine these new birds for around 2 weeks in order to observe them.

However I recall that once I visited someone who claimed to practice strict methods, and who would have been on that list of people I "trust." When I visited the aviary it was plain that a handful of Gouldians were suffering from scaly face mites. I didn't buy anything that day, but if I had I would have introduced mites into the entire aviary!

Closing the aviary

Because of limited space and having only one air supply in the house, I do not enjoy quarantining birds. They currently occupy nearly every room of our house, so it's nearly impossible. Added to that is my belief that the hatchlings/juveniles have enough "work" to do in the matter of growing and molting; they do not need to contract illness or parasites from outside sources. So I 'close' the aviary for certain periods of time. That means I do not bring in any new stock--a self-imposed import restriction -- and I may not let people come in. Some aviaries close to any visitors at all. In this way, one can prevent bringing in disease and simply enjoy the birds.

The Finchly Quarantine Procedure for New Incoming Stock

As soon as a bird arrives, it is checked over and observed in a single cage for a couple of days. We are looking for signs of illness or parasites like fluffing up, and wet or squinted eyes. We are making sure it is eating and drinking, and observing its poo. Note that poo can be 'off' at first, especially if it has spent a day or two traveling to get to us. In general no changes are made at this time. If there is an emergency a little watered-down pedialyte may be given.

Around day 3, begin treatment protocol. Each bird **over 6 months old** gets a drop of Scatt on a bit of bare skin. I like to do it near the nape of the neck, where you put your dog's flea drops. I feel that it is less likely to get rinsed off during a bath, plus they can't preen it back off the feathers. So maybe it sticks around a little better. Another good location is on the skin of the thigh. The Scatt is absorbed into the system via the skin--that's why it's important to put it on the skin--and it will treat for air sac mites and scaly mites for 3 weeks according to the manufacturer.

In addition to the Scatt, I am introducing my feeding regimen of fresh food and egg food, my particular brand of seed, and still observing. After a week or so, you can assume the poo you see is normal for the bird, so it is possible to use it as a diagnostic tool.

The next medication is Ronidasole 12%, which treats canker, giardia and other protozoal infections. Protozoans are not visible to the eye, and they can be insignificant until the finch is burdened with another illness; then their effect becomes multiplied in a sense. *Ronex* (Morning Bird) and *Ronivet-S* (Vetafarm)are the two versions currently available; each is available in either a 6% or a 12% solution. If you do not have the 12% the lower dose can be doubled. Check with the manufacturer to be sure. This has to be administered for 7 consecutive days. I mix it fresh every day into their water. I have only had one finch refuse to drink the water, and the second time I tried (about a month later) he drank it without hesitation.

Next, because Ronidasole does not treat coccidia, it is time to use Baycox. This is given for two days every week for a total of six weeks.

On a day when I have not treated with Baycox, I will give them worm-away. This must be given for 2 consecutive days over 2 weeks. Generally I give a rest day or two between medications.

Disclaimer: This is only my personal schedule; I am not liable for others' use of the plan. If you use this yourself, please do so at your own risk. Check with your veterinarian first.

So here's what the schedule looks like.

Day 3	Scatt on back of neck
Day 7	Begin 1-week Ronex in water
Day 14	End Ronex
Day 18, 19	Treat with Baycox or Medpet 4in1
Day 22	Scatt on back of neck
Day 22, 23	Administer worm-away in water

Day 25, 26	Treat with Baycox or Medpet 4in1
Day 29,30	Administer worm-away in water
Days 32, 33/39, 40/46, 47/53, 54	Treat with Baycox or Medpet 4in1
Day before moving to new quarters	Dip in Avian Insect Liquidator bath

Homework -- because you'll really, really want this later.

Worksheet to Plan For Quarantine

Considering all that you know about quarantine, illness, and parasites, what do you feel is the optimum quarantine period for your personal aviary? _____ days

What length of time does your avian veterinarian recommend? _____ days

Why do you choose to differ your methods from the vet's recommendation? _____

_____

During quarantine, what medications and in what doses will you treat the birds?

List here:

At what point will you consider them healthy enough to join the flock?

When quarantining due to illness, how long will you wait after the bird is deemed healthy before moving it back to the flock?

Allergies

No, not the bird's--I'm talking about yours or someone in your family. All birds have a certain amount of dander, bits of feathers, feather particles, and feather dust that get into the air when birds clean, preen, flap, fly, and poop. When this settles in the house, some remains airborne and travels into human lungs when you breathe. Some people do not even notice allergens; others' bodies respond strongly. Those with mild sensitivity may notice:

Itchy, watery, or swollen eyes, or conjunctivitis (pink eye)
Nasal congestion
Sneezing or coughing, or rhinitis
Scratchy throat
An itchy skin rash

For asthmatics or even people who have mild dander allergies, the allergen can trigger itchy eyes and/or skin and a feeling of the throat "closing up." they may also have a chronic scratchy throat and coughing or wheezing. After that, the lungs may become inflamed. This condition is called alveolitis and may exhibit these symptoms:[xxvi]

- Fever or chills
- Cough
- Muscle pain
- Labored breathing
- Weight loss
- Fatigue

Many people, upon realizing they or a family member have bird allergies, relinquish the bird. This is perhaps not totally necessary. For mild allergies, it is possible to keep it under control by removing the droppings daily; lining the bottom of the cage with disposable liners which are also removed daily; daily vacuuming; using a good air cleaner with a Hepa filter; cleaning every area where the bird has perched; and washing the water container.

For severe allergies or asthma, do all of the above plus

- Wear a face mask when changing the cage
- Consider housing the finches in a room without carpet or curtains; instead, use a washable linoleum and window blinds.
- Vacuum everything in and around the cage daily
- Place a good quality air filter by the cage
- Provide baths for the finches to help them avoid dry skin (which creates more dander)
- Spray down the bedding or newspaper with water before removing to keep the feathers and dander in place while they're being removed.
- Many people also suggest changing the filter on your furnace more often. Purchasing a vacuum cleaner with a Hepa filter will help to clean the air. At my house, we have one dedicated bird room with two air cleaners in place. We have to clean the filter in those every other day.

Another more recent theory for combating allergies or asthma problems is that one can reduce the number of *other* triggers in the environment, in a sense choosing the 'best' one for exposure. For example, people who are allergic to plants and molds can try removing those from the environment and performing the above activities to reduce allergens around the birds.

THE GOULDIAN FINCH HANDBOOK   247

Alternatively, simply increasing the overall cleaning frequency using natural ingredients (vinegar, water, baking soda) instead of commercial cleaners can reduce allergic reactions. You know which allergens are your triggers, so these are just suggestions; the workable solution for reducing allergens will be unique to you.

10 Lists of 10

Ten Awesome Cages that will Delight Your Gouldians

Photos on the website

1. The first cage I have ever seen that's actually longer than recommended:
   King's cage 40X18X13
2. This is the cage most finch owners start with. It is the right size for a pair and has the right bar spacing. To add more pairs, remove one side and place another (with a side removed) against it. Zip tie them together.
   Prevue 30X18X18, 3/8" spacing
   Purchase: http://amzn.to/1EjW2Eh
3. I think this cage is a little small but other people swear by them. They are exceptionally easy to clean, and also keep the seed contained at the bottom.
   Hagen Vision 2 M02, 24X15X34, 1/2" bar spacing https://amzn.to/34WOBbF

THE GOULDIAN FINCH HANDBOOK   249

4. I recommend removing the divider, but it's a nice cage to have around if you must temporarily separate a pair.

> Prevue Hendryx Divided Flight Cage, 24X16X16, 1/2" bar spacing https://amzn.to/376he8Y

5. The best cage I've found, and wish I'd spent the money sooner

> Hampton Deluxe Divided Breeder Cage, 37 1/2" X 18" X 40 1/4" . 1/2" wire spacing. I can't say enough good things about this cage. It's well-made, easy to clean, and you can buy more sets and stack them on top. I currently have 3 sets of double cages, and I do have to stand on a small stool to clean the top one. With the divider out, there's easily room for 4 adult finches or one pair of parrotlets. https://amzn.to/3j08R10

6. McCage 32X19X55. 3/8" bar spacing. 9 feeder doors. It's on wheels and comes in both black and white. https://amzn.to/3o0FOOS

7. Most people I know use this for their larger cage. Prevue F040 31X20X53, 1/2" spacing https://amzn.to/317XHRP

8. I have two of these, and removed one wall to zip tie them together in the center for a total of 72" long. I also liked that there wasn't a lot of space wasted beneath the cage for the shelf area. Use the above link and click XL. Prevue Hendryx X-large 37X23X60, 1/2" bar spacing

9. Awesome cage setup if you know you're going to breed.

> King's Breeder Cage 40X78X13

10. Advantek "The Portico" Aviary. A 41-inch flying space, double "catch" doors – this is a finch owner's dream.

10 Facts About Gouldian Living Quarters

1. To be healthy, birds need to fly
2. A minimum cage size is 30X18X18
3. The cage that cleans up easiest is the best
4. Perches can be clean branches from outdoors, propped across the bars
5. Indoor scented products like candles are deadly to birds
6. Teflon pans when burned give off toxic fumes
7. Outdoor finches must be kept safe from predators
8. Finches like live or fake greenery, it helps them feel safe
9. For health, finches need exposure to sunlight or full spectrum lighting
10. Gouldians do best in 50% or more humidity

10 things to Know and Have Before Breeding

I just finished ranting online at yet another someone who bought a couple of finches, threw them in a cage and gave them a nest immediately after leaving the pet store.

They asked how long it would take for the birds to lay an egg. The poor birds weren't even settled in yet. I suggested the birds might not be old enough to breed, and asked them to feed great nutrition for at least 6 months and go through the quarantine protocol. They came back after a couple days--the nest was now built-- asking how long it takes an egg to hatch.

I get upset when people haven't done their research. I get even more upset when they aren't prepared to deal with possible problems - tossed chicks being the least of them. This hen is probably not physically ready to hatch and rear chicks if she is even old enough to do so.

This list would have been a more sophisticated one, had that incident not just taken place!

1. Know your birds. Know their age, their diet for at least the past 6 months, and their health.
2. Complete the quarantine protocol, or the necessary parts, within 2 to 3 months prior to breeding.
3. Have the right size and type of nest box, baby bird formula, and a syringe (in case of hand feeding) prior to breeding.
4. Extra cages - sometime before, during, or after breeding you will need an extra cage or two. Have those ready.
5. An account with a local veterinarian. If you haven't ever seen the vet, go ahead and set up as a customer with them anyway - preferably with a certified avian vet.
6. Two birds may not be compatible just because you decided to put them together in a cage.
7. Egg laying can take some weeks, it doesn't always happen overnight, in fact -
8. A hen can carry sperm for over a month so if you are picky about which male she's bred to, separate her from the flock before pairing her.
9. Babies that get rejected need hand fed so you need a plan even during work hours for how you will handle that.
10. If you are doing it right you will never make money by breeding birds.

10 Reasons to Provide Appropriate Lighting

1. Light is the vehicle for vitamin production and use
2. It helps keep them on a day/night schedule
3. Light gives birds a sense of seasons
4. Light is needed for full vision
5. It assists in bone development in young chicks
6. It helps laying hens have better health
7. It makes birds more sociable, helping the atmosphere in a multi-bird aviary.
8. Light helps tremendously with proper molting
9. It regulates the endocrine system
10. It contributes to a longer life

See Appendix G for more on lighting

10 Fast Facts about Foods for Finches

1. An all-seed diet is the worst diet.
2. <u>Kale</u> contains large amounts of Vitamin K and folate.
3. <u>Broccoli</u> offers Vitamins A and C and many minerals. The sprouted seeds are better nutritionally than the green vegetable.
4. Lettuce has little nutritional value, but they like it and it provides water.
5. Raw parsley contains a surprising amount of several vitamins and minerals.
6. They love hard boiled egg, including egg shells. Egg is one of the most commonly offered sources of protein. A cup of boiled, chopped egg contains 17 grams of protein. It can be mixed with dry lorikeet mix, canary starter, chick starter, or plain dry bread crumbs for a great supplement.

THE GOULDIAN FINCH HANDBOOK   253

7. Avoid sugary foods; they can cause yeast.
8. You can purchase nutritious bread mix or or make it from scratch
9. Fresh sprouts offer the most nutrition of any food.
10. Every food may be 'suspect' for awhile - repetition is key - keep offering it and they will begin to eat it.
11. Gouldians love fresh cucumber, which may be an aphrodisiac.
12. If you have canaries, provide a small cup of apples and oranges. The canaries will teach the finches how to eat it.

10 Rumors to Lay to Rest

Ahh the rumor mill runs rampant, even in finch world! There are quite a few fallacies floating around. Perhaps we can clear up a few.

All birds that are going to live in a cage your aviary together must be put in at the same time. Although this would be ideal, it's not always possible. If you have a colony of finches that are ready to breed, or that have begun breeding, introducing extra birds in the middle of the season might disrupt the colony and even cause some pairs to stop or abandon their nest. So to set an aviary up properly for breeding, you wouldn't want to introduce an extra pair. However, in general Gouldians are very low-key so I would probably just do a little rearranging in the cage and perhaps add some extra greenery or a new live plant along with the new pair of birds. This is assuming no one is on eggs or feeding brand-new (under one-week-old) babies. This seems to take away the curiosity and everyone adjusts just fine.

If you have too many redheaded birds in the cage, they will be aggressive. This is partially true. Redheaded males, especially the yellow backed ones will be aggressive only during hormone season *in a cage that's large enough for the number of birds*. My suggestion is to double check the size of cage versus the number of birds, and provide more greenery to allow them to feel that they have space. Also, purchasing stress perches or making some will help.

Feeding greens in a large quantity will cause diarrhea. This is partially true, because when a bird eats something with high moisture content like fruit or vegetable, he will *urinate* more due to the water intake. The urine is the clear liquid part of his dropping. So you may think that he's having diarrhea, but it's actually possible for him to urinate without passing any feces along with it. If you are seeing droppings without the white and the green or brown solid part, you're only seeing urine and its normal. Often it's simply more urine than feces, which is polyuria not diarrhea. At any rate, greens are good for him! Unless you've removed all other food and are feeding only greens, I wouldn't worry too much about it.

Gouldians are difficult to keep/breed. Well you only have to look in my cages to know that's not true! I had bird experience, but very little finch experience when I acquired my first 6 finches. They did fine. You have to pay attention, but what pet doesn't require that?

Finches eat only bird seed. No, no and no. By only eating seed, birds will become deficient in many, many nutrients. They will have health problems that you can't solve, and may require expensive veterinary intervention. Please feed your birds fresh vegetables and some of the recipes mentioned in this book along with pellet food and a little seed.

Finches cannot be tamed. This is almost true. The ones that are tame make wonderful little pets. The easiest way to tame one is to pull it from the nest at 10 days

THE GOULDIAN FINCH HANDBOOK   255

- but that will result in you having to hand feed the baby, so I don't recommend it. The second way is to handle them a lot as soon as they hatch, and do it consistently. That way when they fledge, they (hopefully) will remain tame. This isn't a guarantee; sometimes, especially if left in an aviary, they will become wild again. They can be <u>trained</u> in many cases, not to be cuddly but they will go where you tell them and perhaps perch on you. This is sufficient for the large number of people who like to let their bird fly loose.

Gouldians don't raise their own babies. I can tell you that mine do! Sometimes Gouldians toss babies, especially if the parents are very young and inexperienced. It can also be caused by stress (stop checking the nest so often!). It is also possible the clutch has an illness. But in general, Gouldians can and should be good parents.

If my Gouldians toss their babies I can give them to the society finches to raise. This can happen - if a lot of factors are in alignment. The societies need to also be on eggs or hatching babies right around the same time. They will need to accept the Gouldian chicks and be willing to feed them. And there will be a slight disconnect when the society babies fledge at a different time from the Gouldians. It's not as easy as it sounds to make this work.

If you touch a baby bird the mother won't feed it. This may be true of wild birds, but it's not the case with our somewhat domesticated Gouldians. There could be the occasional parent that abandons after someone has handled the babies, but I suspect that has more to do with the baby already having an illness. Handling the babies shouldn't be done too much but it is okay to handle them for nest checks, banding, and cleaning the nest. Just respect the parents and make it quick -- and try not to handle them more than once per day.

Finches are too small to take to the vet. *Au contraire*, there are specialized avian veterinarians who will happily treat your birds. Be sure to locate one before you need their services. A good veterinarian can help you keep your birds healthy and spot nutritional or medical problems that he/she can treat early on, therefore preventing further damage to your little fluff's organs.

23 Varieties that will Peacefully Cohabitate with Gouldians

Wondering what kind of finches you can house alongside your Gouldians? Gouldians are considered a passive finch, and many other species are not. An example is zebra finches; these nervous little birds drive Gouldians crazy, as they never stop moving and will often select a "target" bird to chase or pluck.

House your Gouldians only with types that will not chase or pluck.

Here's a list.

Waxbills:

- Black-cheeked
- Gold-breasted
- Red-eared
- Orange-cheeked
- St. Helena
- Swee

Mannikins & Munia:

- Bronze-winged mannikin
- Chestnut-breasted mannikin
- Chestnut Munia
- Gray-headed Munia

Finches:

- Grass finch
- Pictorella finch
- Quail Finch
- Owl finch
- Painted finch
- Red headed parrot finch
- Blue faced parrot finch (a single pair only)
- Star Finch
- Society Finch
- Silverbills
- Spice finch

Button Quail

Some of these finches would become aggressive if you had more pairs together, or if you were breeding. It's best to relentlessly study the behavior of each species before putting them in the same cage.

Do not EVER place Gouldians in a cage with hookbills, including smaller species. Parrotlets may be the same size but they are notoriously aggressive. The same goes for lovebirds. Many people build a large aviary with the idea of putting several varieties in it. An aviary, though admirable, is still not the same as living in the wild. Many injuries can occur if finches are housed with larger birds.

Ten Sources for Seed, Seed Mixes, Pellets, and Sprouts

Since these resources may change over time, there will be links on the website (https://gouldiangardens.com/book_links)

You might ask, can't I just buy my bird food at the pet store?

Yes you can. I use a popular seed mix, but my local pet store doesn't carry the larger bags so I buy it from Amazon. I can get occasional treats and cockatiel mix locally. I am making these sources available for those who live in more rural areas or people who want to offer better nutrition to their finches.

Birds should not live on a seed-only diet; instead, they need a mix of seeds, pellets, and fresh food.

The best place to get seed mix in bulk is usually Amazon, if you have an Amazon prime account. If not try Chewy.com, which has started carrying more bird items. If there are bird fairs in your area, there are usually vendors there who sell inexpensive bulk mix, but be careful about germs that may be passed there.

People who mix their own insist that the local health food store is the best source for various types of millet, etc. While you're there, pick up some seeds for sprouting.

Otherwise, check these sources:

Seeds for Sprouting

Trueleafmarket.com my current favorite for seeds to plant as well as sprouts

Sproutpeople.org -- many types of sprouts and mixes

Chinaprairie.com - they offer avian kits and two sizes of sprout kits, try the smaller size for finches.

THE GOULDIAN FINCH HANDBOOK   259

Seed Mix

Glam Gouldians - excellent sprout mix and other foods.

Abba Seed - seeds, other food, and cages.

LadyGouldian.com - seed, specialty diets, and medications.

Herman Brothers – Look for finch mix, canary mix, or request your own bulk mix.

Goldenfeast - creates more versions of seed mix than any other company, and it belongs in its own category because theirs is much more than a seed mix. Their Australian blend is a great nutritional source for finches, contains all-fresh ingredients, and includes healthful things like spirulina and bee pollen. If you cannot afford to feed it all the time, I suggest supplying at least a teaspoon now and then.

Pellet food sources

Roudybush has done more testing on birds' diets than anyone, and they have a great product.

Harrison's Organic is another high-quality food; unfortunately, mine won't touch it! I believe you can ask for samples before buying, as I did, 25 pounds of something they won't eat.

Kaytee Exact Rainbow is the inexpensive version of pellet food. Mine won't eat it but I include it here because it is generally available in the big box stores.

TOPS - one of the best sources of nutrition for birds. I like the fact that they cold process, and the birds like the taste. For the finches, I purchase the smaller size and run it in the food processor to grind a little more.

Teas

GreywoodManor.com - This shop carries avian teas that are so important for health. Tea can be made in the traditional method and cooled, or the tea leaves can be sprinkled over their fresh foods.

Ten Fascinating Facts About Gouldian Finches

1. Birds need some UVB rays in order to assist with their vision. If they have rays in the correct range available, they can see the nutrients in their food! To supply the correct range, look for 'full spectrum lighting.' These are fluorescent tubes that contain the same color palette as out door light.

2. In addition to vision, you may have heard that birds need UV rays for their overall health - specifically, to help process vitamin D. Short of regularly spending time outdoors, this is the only way your finches will be able utilize vitamins necessary for bone development, growth, and their mental well-being. Sunlight also assists in regulating the metabolic clock.

3. Finches pick in the droppings on the floor in order to ingest some nutrients they are missing, notably vitamin B12.

THE GOULDIAN FINCH HANDBOOK   261

4. Birds do not breed all year around; there is a definite season. In Gouldians you can tell by looking at a hen's beak. In season, her beak turns black.
5. Lady Gouldians cannot be housed with many kinds of finches because they are too mellow; they are bullied or injured by the more aggressive kinds.
6. Newly hatch Lady Gouldians have luminous nodules, called papillae, near their beaks as well as markings on the inside of their mouths. These markings help direct the parents to the hungry mouths of their chicks in dark nest cavities, their favorite nesting place. Every species of finch has a different arrangement of papillae and mouth markings. As chicks grow, the papillae and markings gradually disappear.
7. Baby Gouldians feather out to a muted olive color, and do not obtain their final coloration until first molt (3 to 12 months).
8. Gouldians are unable to cross breed with most finch species, the exception being the Blue-Faced Parrot Finch (*Erythrura trichroa).*
9. John Gould, a British ornithologist, named the Gouldian after his deceased wife Lady Elizabeth Gould.
10. Gouldians are not only dimorphic (visibly different between genders), but the hens are still beautiful, colorful birds in their own right.

10 Life Saving Natural Remedies

Aloe vera - Fresh aloe treats all wounds on the skin, cere, and even eyes. It will stop bleeding and form a sort of skin over the wound. Slit a piece of aloe down the middle and use the inner gel directly on the bird.

Dandelion - helps with liver troubles and arthritis. Grow fresh plants yourself to ensure no pesticides; serve as part of daily fresh food.

Echinacea augustifolia or purple coneflower is anti-bacterial and works like a high-level antibiotic, according to veterinarian Greg Harrison. Many people use it to build the immune system (their own, not their birds'). Studies show echinacea to be non-toxic. Use the capsule form found in a health food store - mix with water, then add 5 drops to the drinking water. Use for birds with an infection and after antibiotic use.[xxvii]

Egg shells - it is said that if your bird is terribly ill and not eating, they will still eat eggs shells, and this will help them to recover.

Garlic - anti-parasitic and anti-fungal. Use fresh (not the powder form), squeezing the juice into water or mix into fresh foods.

Milk thistle - the best herb to use against liver problems. There are no side effects when using the seeds, which birds love. For finches, it's easier to use an alcohol-free liquid extract, which can be purchased online or in local grocery stores. Use one drop in water, or as your veterinarian recommends.

Neem tea - Neem tea is non-toxic, antimicrobial, anti-fungal, anti-viral, anti-parasitic, and anti-bacterial. It is even effective against air sac mites. Make it by adding boiling water to the leaves and steeping them for an hour, then strain and use the water that's left. However, sometimes birds will not drink it so one must be diligent in watching them. If there are any signs of not drinking (puffiness or lethargy) offer plain water immediately. Neem tea can be used weekly as a preventive.

Neem leaves placed in the bottom of a nest under the nesting material will prevent insects. Neem branches used for perches prevent mites. Neem tea cooled to room temperature can be sprayed on or given as a bath to treat for red mites as well as scaly face mites.

Tulsi (holy basil) - Besides being full of beta-carotene and magnesium, basil can stop quite a few germs such as staphylococcus, enterococcus, and pseudomonas. It's a powerful anti-inflammatory. Birds readily eat it. Use it fresh or frozen.

Turmeric (ground) Grind fresh turmeric and make a paste, put on wounds.

Thyme Thujanol Essential oil (therapeutic grade) diffused near the bird is said to be anti-fungal, anti-viral, and anti-bacterial. Be sure it is *thujanol* which is a milder form of the normally used plant Thymus vulgaris. Use high quality oils only in a high-quality diffuser. Begin with 5 minutes per day of diffusing and build from there. Up to one hour should be safe.

These statements have not been evaluated by the Food and Drug Administration, nor by any veterinarian. All information, including the products and technique mentioned, is for educational purposes only. None of the information is intended to diagnose or treat any disease.

Nontoxic Plants

Plants look so pretty when put in cages or aviaries. It gives a natural feel to the environment, and birds love to hide in the foliage. Note that they also will eat it! Some people are horrified to find their new $25 plant was completely destroyed the first day it was in the aviary. One solution is to have more than one plant and rotate them in and out. Another is to provide small trays of wheatgrass or other edibles that finches like so they'll leave the others alone.

There are so many lists of nontoxic plants online, and from list to list a few items are in conflict with one another.

For example Kalanchoe, one of my favorites, is listed on a popular veterinarian's site as safe. You'd think that would be a great source of information, right? *Kalanchoe is not safe.* So I am choosing to list only the plants I have used in the past in my aviary, which honestly isn't very many. For a comprehensive list, consider speaking to your local extension office or arboretum.

In order to be non-toxic, the plant must not have been sprayed with any chemicals. Also if there is potting soil, consider changing to completely organic; you could also cover it by placing small stones over the soil around the base of the plant. The following are some common plants in the U.S. that are safe for birds.

10 Safe Plants for Aviaries

Aralia & False Aralia	Marigold
Aloe	Peperomia
Baby's tears	Snapdragon
Bamboo	Spearmint
Crimson bottlebrush	Spider Plant
Cucumber, Dill, Garlic	xxviii

Nontoxic Branches for Perches

Many branches are deemed safe if they have not been sprayed with chemicals and if you remove the bark. That sounds like a lot of work to me! I believe these branches are safe, and they are on numerous safe lists:

Apple	Palm
Bamboo	Weeping Willow
Citrus	

30 Toxic Plants to Avoid

Many plants are toxic to birds. Some aloes are toxic, even though aloe lands on most safe lists. Succulents can irritate the digestive system. Here are a few others known for toxic effects on animals.

Azalea
BEANS castor, horse, fava, broad, glory, scarlet runner
Calla Lily
Capsicum (hot pepper)
Clematis
Dieffenbachia
Elderberry
Eggplant (plant, not fruit)
English Holly
Foxglove
Golden Chain Tree
Hydrangea
Jerusalem Cherry
Jimsonweed
Kalanchoe
Lily of the Valley
Mango (wood and leaves, fruit is okay)
Nightshade – all plants
Oleander
Philodendron
Plum
Poinsettia
Rhododendron
Rhubarb leaves
Tobacco
Tomato (plant)
Umbrella Tree
Virginia Creeper
Weeping Fig
Wild Cherry

SAFE Plants for Birds

African violet
Aloe
Areca palm
Australian laurel
Bamboo palm
Begonia

Bird's nest fern
Boston fern
Bottle brush fern
Canary Island palm
Christmas cactus
Coffee tree
Corn plant
Creeping fig

Danish ivy

Devil's ivy
Dragon tree
European fan palm
Ficus benjamina
Fern
Fiddle leaf fig

Fig tree
Flame nettle
Grape Ivy
Herbs, most
Hawaiian schefflera
Indian laurel

American bittersweet
Autumn olive
Bamboo
Barberry
Bayberry
American or
European Beech
Bladdernut
Blueberry
Comfrey
Coralberry
Cotoneaster firethorn
Crabapple
Dogwood
Common, European or
Red Elderberry
Balsam, Douglas,
Subalpine or White Fir
Grape vine
Huckleberry
Marigold
Nasturtium

Ponderosa, Spruce,
Virginia, or White Pine
Pothos
Pyracantha
Raspberry
Rose
Schefflera
Swedish Ivy

Jade plant	Snowberry
Kangaroo vine	Black, Norway, Red, or White Spruce
Lace fern	Viburnum
Lady palm	Wax plant
Maidenhair fern	White poplar
Ming fern	Willow
Mother fern	Zebra Plant
Mother-in-law's tongue	
Norfolk pine	
Paradise palm	
Parlor palm	
Pepperomia	
Prayer plant	
Purple passion	
Rubber tree	
Spider plant	
Umbrella tree	

End

Thank you for reading my book. Before closing it, would you take a moment or two to leave a review on Amazon, Goodreads, or wherever you bought it? It would mean so much to me.

A review doesn't have to be long or detailed; the purpose is to share your opinion, so that others can decide if the book is valuable to them. Thanks – I really appreciate it.

Whenever a new book or training resource is released, I offer my mailing list members advance notice and an exclusive offer. If you would like to receive that notification, please visit https://GouldianGardens.com/join.

And of course if you haven't gotten a copy of my book *Feeding Finches*, please do grab one soon.

Acknowledgements

As they say, it takes a village to write a book. I can't begin to list all the people who have helped, encouraged, read, and edited my book. I'm going to try.

Many thanks for the patience of my veterinarians and my "bird" friends. I am especially grateful to those who have made suggestions, read through the manuscript, and contributed ideas or photos.

My thanks to the NFSS staff who encouraged me to keep going on this project. My parents, brother, and children are the most supportive family anyone could every want. I owe so much to my beta reader group: Mary Ann Farmer, Tamara Hager, Dianne Allen, Jan Croft, Donnie Fear, Claire Jacobs, and Rick Coffman. Most of all I owe so much to my husband Mickey, who stands behind me when I need support and in front of me when I need encouragement. He is my rock.

The pictures and illustrations in the book are mostly my own. Others as noted have come from Tina Billings, Cornel Volschenk, Patrick Platon, and Lisa Judson-Bohard.

About the Author

Tanya Logan is an aviculturist experienced with many bird species, but Gouldians remain her favorite. She is a former news columnist and former editor of the National Finch and Softbill Society Journal. Tanya holds an M.A. in Education. She and her husband Mickey reside in Southwest Florida with a diverse flock. They are nothing but bird slaves.

More Books by this Author

The Congenial Cockatiel, A Complete Guide to Owning, Housing and Breeding America's Favorite Pet Bird (planned release date 2021)

Feeding Finches for Health and Longevity (2020)

Come Back to Jesus, and Don't Bring Your Blackberry (2013)

How to Be Your Own Contractor and Save Thousands While Keeping Your Day Job (2008)

How to Open & Operate a Financially Successful Construction Company (2008)

The Real Estate Developer's Handbook (2007)

Appendix A

GLOSSARY

Allele: Any possible form of a gene.

Autosomal: Any characteristic (chromosome) that is not a sex chromosome.

Chromosome Pair: A pair that are similar in function and form. Chromosomes are always present in pairs, the exception being sex chromosomes. They may vary in genetic composition because of differences in the alleles at matching loci on the pair.

Dominant: A Genetic Factor expressed in the phenotype even when only one copy is present. Example - AA and Aa are expressed visually the same way, as the dominant A.

Fledge: When baby birds emerge from the nest for the first time.

Genotype: The entire genetic makeup, including the traits that are not physically shown--like the 'split', I.e., split to white breast or split to orange head.

Heterozygous: Having two different alleles at the same loci on a chromosome pair. Example: purple breast and white breast Pw. We can call this single factor if referring to autosomal traits.

Homozygous: Having two identical genes at the same loci on a chromosome pair. If referring to sex-linked traits in cock birds, we say double factor. Hens cannot be double factor.

Incomplete Dominance: A genetic factor will be partially expressed. Example -- a brindle dog and a white dog mate, the offspring are patchy white and brindle.

Locus (singular) or loci (plural): The location of a gene, or its allele, on a chromosome. All Chromosome pairs have matching loci.

Phenotype: The trait that is expressed (purple breast, red head, etc.).

Recessive: A gene that is only expressed when present on both loci of a pair.

Sex-linked: Characteristics present on a sex chromosome, so that they are single- or double-factor in cock birds but only SF in hens.

Sitting Tight: When a hen begins incubating her eggs, usually after 3+.

Split: Usually describes the hidden trait in a heterozygous pair. Shown with a /.

Appendix B

AN ENDANGERED SPECIES

The Gouldian finch is considered an endangered species because in its native land, Australia, there are a mere 2,500 mature Gouldians in the wild. There are tiny populations in Western Australia and in the Northern Territory.

It is thought that the decline is due to the changes in land use-- grazing livestock on open pasture prevents grass from going to seed. Wildfires and parasites are also a problem.

What can be done?

The Australian government and the World Wildlife Fund are working on restoring the habitats and re-introducing Gouldians to their native areas. Part of their work includes extensive nutritional research, remote tracking, and a nestbox project. Due to fewer and fewer hollow trees, nest boxes are necessary to encourage Gouldians to reproduce.

How can I help?

Breeding and selling Gouldians in the U.S. is *not* the answer to the habitat problem in Australia! Gouldians will not survive if you liberate them in the U.S. They are susceptible to predators and weather, and they've been captive-bred long enough that they lack the natural instinct to locate food and water.

The best way we can help with the Australian efforts is by donating to their charity effort, http://savethegouldian.net/ . Just a small donation goes a long way for a pair of finches.

Appendix C

FULL SPECTRUM LIGHTING

Lights seem to be a mystery for some, but they don't need to be. Bulbs that say "full spectrum" at the hardware store will be good, as are avian-specific lights found online. Remember that lights must be within a certain distance to be effective; using clip-on fixtures or mounting lights nearest the food containers will help.

To set the timer, think about what season it is in your aviary. Some people are manipulating theirs, which is why the question isn't "which season it is in your hemisphere." If staggering the lights to simulate sunrise or sunset, set several timers about 10 minutes apart.

For the fall/winter, austerity, or non-breeding season, lighting can be reduced to 10-12 hours. Birds often have a natural set time they go to roost, so that could be the beginning of lights out.

When transitioning to the breeding season, slowly being increasing daylight hours by 10 minutes a day or 30 minutes weekly – whatever works for you. Stop when you reach 13 or even 14 hours. In the natural Gouldian habitat, daylight only increases to about 13 hours.

Lighting can also be used to offset hens that are chronic egg layers. Reducing the light hours slowly as mentioned above can help to lower the hormones and help her stop laying.

Appendix D

FORMS AND DOCUMENTS

Individual Bird Record

[photo]

Hatched: / /   Sex: C H

Band(s): _____

Mutation
    Phenotype:
    Genotype:

Lineage:

Cock	
Hen	Cock
Cock	
Hen	Hen

Origin:

_____
_____

Acquired on: __/_____/ _____ **Acquired from:** _____

_____
_____

Medical History: - note all treatments and medications

_____
_____
_____

Notes

_____
_____
_____

Breeding Records

Clutch Breeding Record

Dates bred: _____ / _____ / _____ Clutch#: _____ Cage: _____ ID: _____

Sire: Head color: _____
    Breast color: _____
    Back color: _____
    Band # _____

Dam: Head color: _____
    Breast color: _____
    Back color: _____
    Band # _____

First Egg Laid: Incubation: **Fledge:**   **Chicks Weaned:**

	# Eggs Laid:	Fertile:	Hatched:	Survived:

Chick ID	Hatch Date	Mutation	Sex	Notes
	/			
	/			
Chick ID	Hatch Date	Mutation	Sex	Notes
	/			
	/			
Chick ID	Hatch Date	Mutation	Sex	Notes
	/			
	/			
Chick ID	Hatch Date	Mutation	Sex	Notes
	/			
	/			
Chick ID	Hatch Date	Mutation	Sex	Notes
	/			
	/			
Chick ID	Hatch Date	Mutation	Sex	Notes
	/			
	/			

Breeding Set-up: _____

Cage ID: _____   **Notes:** _____

Bibliography

Axelson, R., & Axelson, C. (n.d.). Finches - Feeding. Retrieved September 06, 2020, from http://www.vca-hospitals.com/main/pet-health-information/article/animal-health/finches-feeding/867.

Beaudoin, Terry. The Necessity of Full-Spectrum Light, http://www.parrotislandinc.com/articles/alight.htm. Accessed 10/1/17.

Burgmann, P. M. (1993). Feeding your pet bird. Hauppauge, NY: Barron's.

Evans, S. and Fidler, M., 2005. The Gouldian Finch. New Farm, Queensland: Indruss Productions.

Fidler, Mike. Fostering, *Just Finches & Softbills*, Issue 25.

Fidler, Mike. Sprouting: Finch Society of Australia (FSA) at finchsociety.org *sorry, this site seems to have disappeared before I got the full notation.

Finch Care and Diseases, http://australianfinches.com/FinchCare/Diseases.aspx.

Food breakdowns courtesy of http://nutritiondata.self.com/

Ghaly AE and Alkoaik FN. The Yellow Mealworm as a Novel Source of Protein. *American Journal of Agricultural Biological Science* 2009; 4(4):319-331.

Harrison, Gregg, and Lightfoot, Theresa (Ed.), Clinical Avian Medicine (Vol. 2, pp. 879-914). Palm Beach, FL: Spix Publishing.

Highfill, Carol. A Bit About Grit: Do Birds Need It? (June 1, 2001), http://www.birdsnways.com/wisdom/ww58eii.htm

Kaufmann, J. Arthropods. *Parasitic Infections of Domestic Animals: A Diagnostic Manual* (P.374-376). Germany: Springer, 1996.

Kingston, R. J. (2010). The finch: A breeder's companion. Queensland, Australia: Indruss Productions.

Low, R. (2006). THE PARROT COMPANION. London, UK: New Holland.

Pryke, Sarah R., & Simon C. Griffith, *Science,* Vol. 323, Issue 5921, (20 Mar 2009). pp. 1605-1607.

Ritchie, B. W., Harrison, G. J., & Harrison, L. R. (1994). Avian medicine: Principles and applications. Lake Worth, FL: Wingers.

Sakas, P., DVM. (2006) and P. Coutteel DVM. Chapter 39: Management of Canaries, Finches, and Mynahs. In 917498524 720997104

Some Common Avian Diseases, Medpet Company, http://www.medpet.co.za/news/common-avian-diseases_Apr2008.htm

Taylor, M. A., Coop, R. L., & Wall, R. L. Part 1: General Parasitology. In *Veterinary Parasitology* (pp. 227-229). Chichester, West Sussex: Wiley Blackwell, 2013.

Tidemann, S. (2010, May 11). Causes of the decline of the Gouldian Finch Erythrura gouldiae. Retrieved September 06, 2020, from http://journals.cambridge.org/action/displayAbstract?fromPage=online originally published Conservation Commission of the Northern Territory, P.O. Box 496, Palmerston, NT 0831, Australia http://www.abc.net.au/catalyst/stories/2589683.htm

Vriends, M. M. (1996). Hand-feeding and raising baby birds: Breeding, hand-feeding, care, and management. New York, NY: Barron's Educational Series.

Endnotes

1. Printing industry switch to soy-based ink not set on paper, Edmundo Conchas and M. Steele Brown, Feb, 27, 2000, San Antonio Business Journal , https://www.bizjournals.com/sanantonio/stories/2000/02/28/focus2.html accessed 6/2/19.
2. https://www.britannica.com/science/preen-gland, Accessed 3/7/17.
3. Grassfinches, p. 34
4. Uptake Of Ingested Calcium During Egg Production In The Zebra Finch (Taeniopygia G Uttata), S. James Reynold, The Auk 114(4):562-569, 1997.
5. https://ladygouldian.com/content/endocox, accessed 6/21/2018.

[i] https://shorturl.at/lqIY9 Pet Business, Poison Prevention, ROBYN BRIGHT, Published: 06.30.2015
[ii] https://www.forthebirdsdvm.com/blogs/news/1586482-whats-that-cage-made-of
[iii] Dumonceaux, G. (1997). Toxins. In 959597554 746837947 R. H. Harrison (Author), Avian medicine: Principles and Application (pp. 566-584). Lake Worth, FL: Wingers.

[iv] Jaskulski, L., RVT. (2010, October). Disinfection -- Principles, Methods and Madness. Retrieved September 30, 2020, from http://www.mickaboo.com/newsletter/oct10/Disinfecting.html October 2010 Newsletter, Mickaboo Bird Rescue Companion.

[v] Margaret A. Wissman, DVM. (2006). 20 Things You Must Know About Nutrition. Retrieved September 03, 2016, from http://exoticpetvet.net/avian/20facts.html.

[vi] https://www.finchsociety.org.

[vii] Shephard, M., Forshaw, J. and Pridham, A., 2012. Grassfinches In Australia. [S.l.]: CSIRO PUBLISHING, pp.21-24.

[viii] "Raw Millet per 100 g, Food Report," FoodData Central 169702. Retrieved October 07, 2020, from https://fdc.nal.usda.gov/fdc-app.html.

[ix] Fidler, Mike. A New Way of Sprouting Seed. https://www.fabulousfinch.com/index.php?_route_=how-to-sprout-seed-for-birds.html

[x] Rickman, J., Barrett, D., & Bruhn, C. (2007, March 14). Nutritional comparison of fresh, frozen and canned fruits and vegetables. Part 1. Vitamins C and B and phenolic compounds. Retrieved September 06, 2020, from https://onlinelibrary.wiley.com/doi/abs/10.1002/jsfa.2825.

[xi] Hunter, K., & Fletcher, J. (2002, October 03). The antioxidant activity and composition of fresh, frozen, jarred and canned vegetables. Retrieved September 06, 2020, from https://www.sciencedirect.com/science/article/pii/S1466856402000486

[xii] ABC News, S. (2017, May 13). Are fresh vegies always better than frozen? Retrieved September

06, 2020, from https://www.abc.net.au/news/health/2017-05-14/fresh-vs-frozen-vegies/8443310

[xiii] Orak, H., Aktas, T., Yagar, H., İsbilir, S., Ekinci, N., & Sahin, F. (2012, August). Effects of hot air and freeze drying methods on antioxidant activity, colour and some nutritional characteristics of strawberry tree (Arbutus unedo L) fruit. Retrieved September 06, 2020, from https://www.ncbi.nlm.nih.gov/pubmed/22522307

[xiv] https://www.ncbi.nlm.nih.gov/pubmed/3155617. This report does show a correlation between lupus in monkeys and alfalfa sprouts.

[xv] Fabulous Finches on YouTube, https://www.youtube.com/channel/UCejbdmRt5xqNw0ZjzEFBWaQ.

[xvi] Mealworms as Food, (March 1, 2011), http://abigalesedibles.com/mealworms-as-food/.

[xvii] Pryke, S., & Griffith, S. (n.d.). The relative role of male vs. female mate choice in maintaining assortative pairing among discrete colour morphs. Retrieved September 06, 2020, from https://pubmed.ncbi.nlm.nih.gov/17584244/. J. Evol. Biol. 20, 1512–1521 (2007).

[xviii] Buransky, M. (2016, September 22). Gouldian finch. Retrieved June 29, 2019, from http://www.gouldianfinches.eu/en/genetics/genetics-and-mutations-in-gouldian-finches/how-plumage-colors-are-made/.

[xix] Sakas, P. S., MD. (n.d.). Evaluation of Bird Droppings-An Indicator of Health. Retrieved from https://nilesanimalhospital.com/files/2012/05/The-Dropping-_-An-Indicator-of-Health.pdf

288   TANYA LOGAN

[xx] Fidler, Mike. Baldness in Gouldians. https://www.naturallyforbirds.com.au/bald-gouldlians. Accessed 09/27/20.

[xxi] Harrison, R. H. (1997). Viruses. In Avian medicine: Principles and application (p. 509). Lake Worth, Florida: Wingers.

[xxii] Merck Veterinary Manual. (2020, January). Nutritional Disorders of Pet Birds. https://www.merckvetmanual.com/bird-owners/disorders-and-diseases-of-birds/nutritional-disorders-of-pet-birds?query=calcium.

[xxiii] Black, R. (2017, April 12). Carbohydrates – The Good and Bad Points - NFSS: National Finch & Softbill Society. Retrieved September 06, 2020, from https://nfss.org/education/articles/carbohydrates-the-good-and-bad-points/

[xxiv] University of Eastern Finland. (2019, January 15). Effects of linoleic acid on inflammatory response depend on genes. ScienceDaily. Retrieved September 6, 2020 from www.sciencedaily.com/releases/2019/01/190115124500.htm.

[xxv] Balanced Omega Fatty Acids: Why Do Birds Need Them? (2018, June 19). Lafeber Company. https://lafeber.com/pet-birds/balanced-omega-fatty-acids-why-do-birds-need-them/

[xxvi] http://www.wingwise.com/droppings.htm

[xxvii] Ritchie, B. W., Harrison, G. J., & Harrison, L. R. (1999). Avian Medicine: Principles & Applications (1st ed.). HBD International, Inc.

[xxviii] Compiled from Peterson, M. E., & Talcott, P. A. (2013). Household and Garden Plants. In Small animal toxicology (pp. 397-398). St. Louis, MO: Elsevier/Saunders.

CPSIA information can be obtained
at www.ICGtesting.com
Printed in the USA
BVHW061050210222
629654BV00006BA/431